Quentin Crisp

is 'in the profession of being'. He has written, in his spare time, *The Naked Civil Servant, How to Become a Virgin* and *Manners from Heaven*. Donald Carroll, who edited these diaries, also worked thirty years ago on *The Naked Civil Servant* and is co-author of Crisp's *Doing It with Style*.

QUENTIN CRISP

Resident Alien

The New York Diaries

Flamingo
An Imprint of HarperCollins*Publishers*

Flamingo
An Imprint of HarperCollins*Publishers*
77–85 Fulham Palace Road,
Hammersmith, London W6 8JB

Published by Flamingo 1997
9 8 7 6 5 4 3 2 1

First published in Great Britain by
HarperCollins*Publishers* 1996

ISBN 0 00 638717 9

Set in Aldus

Printed and bound in Great Britain by
Caledonian International Book Manufacturing Ltd, Glasgow

CONTENTS

1993

1994

INTRODUCTION

Some years ago the American journalist and editor Willie Morris wrote a fine memoir called *North Toward Home* in which he described his motives, and his experiences, in leaving Mississippi to live in New York City. With that precedent in mind, it occurred to me that perhaps these journals should be called *West Toward Home*. Eventually I rejected the idea – just as, thirty years ago, when I was editing Quentin's autobiography, I vetoed the idea of calling it *I Reign in Hell*, preferring instead his alternative title, *The Naked Civil Servant*. With the present volume I decided against *West Toward Home* because Quentin's homing instincts are fixed on people, not places. Indeed, when we first met he confided, 'I don't hold with abroad' – adding, for emphasis, 'I know, for example, the French speak English when our backs are turned.'

So for this most English of Englishmen (whatever he may say) to uproot himself, in his seventies, and move from London to New York required, above all, exceptional courage. This means his move came as no surprise to those of us who know him well, because we know him to be, above all, a man of courage. To dare to be different, in whatever context, takes a certain amount of courage. To *parade* yourself as different, in *every* context, takes an extraordinary amount of courage. To do it wittily is to invite the constant possibility of being lynched.

Yet Quentin has now lived for fifteen years in one of Manhattan's most insalubrious neighbourhoods – the Lower East Side, hard by the Bowery – alongside drug dealers, pimps, derelicts, Hell's Angels and all manner of low life, without ever having been assaulted or even threatened. He has lived all those years with a listed telephone number and yet receives fewer crank calls than the average housewife in Kansas City. And he has only once been stopped by the New York police: they wanted to know how his one-man show was going, and to wish him well with it.

What accounts for this unique exemption from all the menaces and hassles that the rest of us would undoubtedly suffer were we to live as he lives, where he lives? His own explanation, typically, omits any mention of himself: it is entirely due to the friendliness and tolerance of others. Which may be true, but which misses the point. The point is that the friendliness and tolerance his presence inspires is *reflected* friendliness, *mirrored* tolerance. Although he would probably laugh uproariously at the notion, the fact is that it is almost impossible to behave badly in his company.

I know. In 1981 we were sent by our American publishers on a three-week authors' tour of the US to promote our book, *Doing It with Style*. For three weeks we travelled everywhere together, waited in airports together, attended book signings together, appeared on more than sixty radio and television programmes together, spent hours in hotel rooms together, ate every meal together. Now, anyone who has ever been on holiday with friends for three weeks knows that it is the acid test of one's capacity for friendship; likewise, anyone who has ever been on a promotional tour knows that it is the ultimate test of one's ability to remain sane in a landscape of unreality. Yet we survived our ordeal not only with our friendship intact, but with my having been given a master class in courtesy and good manners.

One example will suffice. At the end of a particularly gruelling day, at the end of a gruelling week, we had collapsed in our suite at the Chateau Marmont in Los Angeles when the telephone rang. Quentin answered it and, after covering the handset, whispered the name of someone I most definitely did not wish to speak to. 'Say I'm not here, say I'm dead, say anything,' I growled.

Quentin nodded, and then spoke soothingly into the telephone: 'I'm afraid Mr Carroll can't come to the phone at the moment, but if you are willing to talk to me I will say exactly what he would have said.' The caller was instantly charmed; I was suitably chastened.

On a later occasion in New York – all right, two examples will suffice – we were being approached by a young man all aglow with a terrible earnestness when I suggested that we beat a hasty retreat to avoid the likelihood of being bored unto death. Unmoved, and unmoving, Quentin quietly corrected me: 'No one is boring who is willing to tell the truth about himself.' That was when I realized just what it was that gave him the *sauf-conduit* which to this day allows him to pass unmolested through the dimmest alleyways of the *demi-monde*. It is his willingness, at all times, in all circumstances, to tell the truth – the whole truth – about himself.

Of course if that was all there was to it, I would be writing here about an unfailingly honest and decent old man who richly deserves the solicitude of his neighbours. Instead I am writing about a man admired and celebrated throughout the English-speaking world. What links the two, and incorporates the former into the latter, is, as everybody knows, his coruscating wit – his almost alchemical wizardry in converting seemingly lacklustre truths into lustrous *aperçus*. It is no exaggeration to say that Quentin Crisp could well be the wittiest man alive.

For that very reason, unfortunately but understandably, he is often spoken of as the Oscar Wilde *de nos jours*. The comparison, however well-intentioned, does Quentin a disservice. For Oscar Wilde, wit was a weapon, a duelling sword with which he could take on all comers and defeat them with his swordplay. For Quentin, wit is more a magic wand of revelation – no less rapier-like than Wilde's, no less glinting in the sunlight of retelling, but waved gently rather than brandished. Because Wilde never came to terms with the truth about himself, because he was for ever trying to graft his persona on to his person, he used his wit to score points off those who would challenge him. Quentin, on the other hand, with no secrets to keep from himself or others, no territory to defend, has always used his wit to embrace the world that now, at last, so enthusiastically embraces him. As a result, whereas Wilde was reduced to wallowing in lachrymose self-pity and writing mawkish verse until his lonely death at the age of forty-six, Quentin at the age of eighty-six is still cheerfully holding the door open for latecomers to his party.

Do come in. I promise you a good time.

DONALD CARROLL
London, Spring 1995

I Serve in Heaven

I never had much luck with titles.

The Naked Civil Servant was a terrible title. Everywhere I go, I find myself compelled to explain it – to describe how a feature writer for an obscure paper visited me once in my room in Chelsea to ask me if I was a famous model for artists and I told him that there was no such thing, that by the time I entered that profession, art had become 'non-figurative', that in a time outworn, when they had nothing better to write about, journalists descended on Chelsea and asked some girl, who spent her time in The Pheasantry in a black velvet dress with one shoulder bare, if she slept with Mr John or Mr Epstein or whoever or only sat for him, that now 'life drawing' was only done – and done reluctantly – by students in art schools, and that the model arrived at the same time every day, that he presented his employment card, signed on and off and was frequently paid by a cheque which came from the Minister of Education – that, in other words, being a model had become as humdrum as being a civil servant, except that you had no clothes.

I had wanted to call my life story *I Reign in Hell*, which seemed to me a self-evident title. Mr Milton recounts how Satan (who is my only role model) had said 'better to reign in Hell than serve in Heaven,' which is what I had done – reigned in the exciting hell of Soho instead of serving in the boring heaven of Kensington. Had I been allowed to use that title for my autobiography, these journals would be called *I Serve in Heaven*, for Manhattan has far exceeded my expectation of happiness.

When I arrived in America, with all my worldly goods tied up in a red handkerchief, I was betrayed. In 1980, I had met a man who had said I could stay with him indefinitely when I arrived. I wrote to him from England telling him of the day and almost the hour of my arrival on the other side of the world. He had not replied so I had assumed that he was waiting for me. He was not. Indeed, he did not even open the door of his apartment but made inaudible replies to my announcement of my presence, so I went to my only other friend in America, a man who had constituted himself my 'manager' while I tarried in Manhattan during the previous year. So I lived in unaccustomed and uneasy splendour on 39th Street for the first six weeks of my life in America.

This man and his little friend were part-time saints because I slept in their living room, which curtailed their social life severely, but they never complained, never made me feel unwelcome. But it was a great relief to all concerned when one of my spies found me the room I now occupy on Manhattan's Lower East Side. This is an ideal spot, though guests look round the place uneasily and say, 'Do you *have* to live here?' I reply, 'Yes' – but that is not the whole truth. If I knew that I would die sometime during the next two years, I could live in a palace riddled with standard of living, but unfortunately I don't. I never dreamed that I would live as long as I have. When I was young, everybody said, 'We never thought you'd live through another winter' and that was nice. It made me feel frail, not long for this world, but here I am, a somewhat grisly sight, tottering about the Lower East Side of Manhattan at the age of eighty-six. When I got to America I hoped I would die before my shoes wore out but now my entire wardrobe is threadbare and I am threadbare too.

There is a strange relationship between the system of a country and its people. In England, the people are hostile to a man but the system is compassionate. The very old, the very young and the ill-equipped-to-live will always be looked after. In America everyone is friendly – almost doggie-like – but the system is ruthless. Once you can be pronounced unproductive, you've had it. You will end up living in a cardboard box at the corner of a street where once you occupied a mansion. That is the reason why I live in one room in a rooming house on the same block as a group of Hell's Angels. They have a bad reputation, but they've never murdered me. When I take my washing to the Chinese laundry on First Avenue, I pass between their house and the row of Harleys marshalled outside it. I walk with bowed head to show that I respect their supremacy and they leave me alone.

My mode of living only represents poverty to Americans – not to me. I live here in exactly the same way that I lived in London. I like living in one room and have never known what people do with the room they are not in. The only trouble is the books. I try never to read. Books are for writing, not for reading, but still they pursue you from three sources. Firstly, authors send you the books they have written. I don't think English writers ever do that. It would seem immodest. These you must read for fear that you will meet their authors on the street and they will question you about their work. Then there are the magazines that send you books with a covering note telling how many words to write about them and what you will be paid. Lastly, there are publishers who send you uncorrected proof copies of books they intend to market with a letter that says, 'We are sure you will enjoy this book and hope you will share your enthusiasm with us.' That means: 'Say something nice that we can put on the back of the first edition. Do not expect to be paid.' To these I always reply, 'Please feel free to quote me as saying anything that will promote sales of this excellent work.' Mostly the publishers do just that. One firm quoted the whole line, which I thought was really daring and funny.

In spite of the march of the books across the carpet, there is still room for a chair, a bed, a cooking stove and a refrigerator. What more can you ask? Rents *are* high here. My room in London, where I lived for forty-one years, cost six pounds a week. My room here is seventy-five dollars a week. All this happiness has to be paid for.

*   *   *

I have always been American in my heart, ever since my mother took me to the pictures (silent). She did this in a spirit of ostentatious condescension. Films, she said, were for servant gels. Anyone with any taste went to the theatre. When I began to gibber with excitement, she warned me that movies were greatly exaggerated – that America was nothing like it was portrayed on the screen. I suspected that she was wrong and that everyone over here was beautiful and everyone was rich.

Though not everyone is rich, everyone *is* beautiful. This is due to the addition of a Mediterranean ingredient. For instance, in the district where I live, Spanish is spoken. The shopkeepers speak American to you but they gibber away in their native tongue to one another. Those who are not Spanish are Greek or Italian. That means that their lips are curly, their nostrils are flared, their eyelids are as thick as pastry. When I was only English, I asked an American soldier if he thought there was an English face. Immediately he said Yes. Then I asked if it looked as though there was not enough material to go round. To this he also agreed. The English have flap lips, papery eyelids, prominent jawbones and Adam's apples. We are an ill-favoured race. I recognize that now that I live here.

A huge man sitting next to me on a bus going up Third Avenue asked me if I lived here permanently. When I said that I did, he remarked, 'It is the place to be if you are of "a different stripe".' There are so many different nationalities, so many different income groups, so many different sexes, that the freaks pass unnoticed. People have always imagined, or pretended to imagine, that I seek to provoke hostile attention. This is rubbish. What I want is to be accepted by other people without bevelling down my individuality to please them – because if I do that, all the attention, all the friendship, all the hospitality that I receive is really for somebody else of the same name. I want love on my own terms.

Here I have it. I was standing on Third Avenue waiting for a bus when a black gentleman walked by. When he noticed me, he said, 'Well, my! You've got it all on today.' And he was laughing.

In London, people stood with their faces six inches from mine and hissed, 'Who do you think you are?' What a stupid question. It must have been obvious that I didn't think I was anybody else.

People are my only pastime. I do not walk about the streets lost in thought about some problem of politics or mathematics or philosophy, so no one interrupts my train of thought by speaking to me. I welcome them. When we say of anyone that he is boring, it is ourselves we are criticizing. We have not made ourselves into that wide, shallow vessel into which a stranger feels he can pour anything. I have said that no one is boring who will tell the truth about himself. Here people tell the truth – or what they perceive as the truth – because they know that nothing they might say will shock or disgust me or cause me to despise them. They tell me their life stories at street corners while waiting for the traffic lights to change, because, like everyone in America who has been on television, I wear in public an expression of fatuous affability.

In other words, I have gone into the fame business. My agent tells me that I can't just 'do' fame, but I can. Every day through the mails I receive what is crudely called junk mail. It consists of invitations to Broadway theatre first nights, to secret screenings of unpopular films, to the openings of galleries exhibiting works of obscure artists and to parties for someone no one has ever heard of in dim basements. I can't go to all of them but I must go to some or they will cease to send them and I shall be cut off from the world. They serve a dual purpose. They keep me in touch with the press – and, if I can live on peanuts and champagne, I need never buy food again. I have learned not to flinch at the flashes from the cameras and to nod when I have not heard what is being said. That is all I need to know.

I never refuse to be photographed. That is no easy thing, as every fifth person in Manhattan is a professional photographer, and I never refuse to answer questions, however trivial they may be. One woman rang me at seven-thirty in the morning and asked me how to prevent her lipstick from smearing. Another wanted me to tell her what to do because she had allowed her hairdresser to cut her hair short and now she had decided that she didn't like it.

When I go on television, I remember that there only one law prevails: the survival of the glibbest. If your interviewer asks the question, 'What is the secret of the universe?', you do not stutter, you do not hesitate, above all you do not say, 'A good question.' You say, with a gracious smile, 'I am happy to tell you there is no secret.' The remark is inane, but you are smiling and your lips are moving. You'll be back.

All this is very tiring but not working is always hard work, and it has its rewards. Your travel expenses and your hotel expenses are taken care of. This does not mean that you see America. You see the airport. You see the hotel. You see the university or lecture hall. That is all, but you went to some delightful metropolis to be seen rather than to see.

I have actually seen – in the sense that I have roamed about the city – Seattle, which is as far west as you can go (except Alaska, which heaven forfend). I have seen Grosse Pointe, a Doris Day district which forms a suburb of Detroit. When you eat in Detroit, the restaurant turns while you dine. When you have reached the pudding, you are over a river called the Detroit River. When I asked my hostess what lay beyond the river, she replied, 'Canada'. So I reckoned that I was as far north as I could go (still not mentioning Alaska). I have also been to the southern extremity of the United States, to Key West. It is a purely holiday island. No one ever works there. It is full of guest-houses, piano bars and restaurants, and everyone wears white. It is a shrine to Mr Hemingway. Every bar shows proudly his photograph with the words, 'Hemingway drank here' – or 'slept here' – or 'fought here' – or 'wrote here'. All these places and many others I have visited with my fare paid both ways and my hotel bill taken care of. I have generally been given, if not the keys of the cities, at least the impression that I am welcome.

I would not go on so much about this aspect of my life if it were not in such contrast with my previous experience. I have been to a lot of places but I have not spent much time away from home because each visit to a distant city is of such short duration. I travel thousands of miles to be away only for three days. As I never travel with any luggage that I cannot carry on to the plane with me, this suits me fine. I do not find air travel tiring because I sleep on planes, following the advice of Miss Eartha Kitt, who said, 'On a plane, never eat, never drink. Sleep.' Thus I do not suffer from jet-lag. It is my guess that people who say they have jet-lag are the people who start to drink before the wretched plane has got its feet off the ground and who arrive at their destination with scarlet faces and crooked hats. They've got gin-lag.

I am met at the airport. It is like being a spy. If no one is there to meet me, I can only return home again for I have no idea where I am going. So far this has never happened. I have also no idea what I am expected to do. On being asked this question, my hosts sometimes say breezily, 'Oh, nothing really. Just enjoy yourself and be there.' Sometimes I am expected to sign books, sometimes to talk to people, answer questions, be photographed. It is very moving – the love that Americans shower upon you, their gratitude for your presence.

In San Francisco, however, the only American city in which I have ever received totally bad notices, the critics could see how overcome I was and made fun of me. I think my reception there was due to an expectation that I was somebody who went about the world hiring spaces in which to deliver a manifesto. When I explained that I myself was hired and that, as far as I knew, my function was to sell theatre seats and that, furthermore, in my opinion, every theatre-goer throughout the world was a middle-class middle-aged woman with a broken heart, the people of San Francisco's love for me died in an instant. In other cities, I have fared better – noticeably in New York and Los Angeles.

It is very stimulating to work in Los Angeles because when you look down into the audience you see that the theatre is full of movie stars. I once signed books there in the interval of my show and when one person placed his book before me I said, 'And what is your name?' 'Roddy,' he replied. I wrote 'Roddy' and he added 'McDowall'. 'You're Roddy McDowall!' I cried in ecstasy. 'You remember me?' he asked, and I certainly did. 'You divorced Lassie,' I said to prove it. I think he must be the most famous person that I have ever met – except Mr Sting. Because I was in a movie with Mr Sting, when I played his laboratory assistant and he was Baron Frankenstein, people imagine that I see him incessantly, whereas I have met him only twice – once when he took me to lunch in a restaurant on West Broadway and told me he was going to write songs about exiles, and again when I was in his videotape of the song about being an Englishman in New York. Then he took me into his apartment, which was a huge place almost entirely bare of furniture, except that in one room I noticed a cot: evidence of Stinglets. I did not comment on this fact, fearing to embarrass him.

Mr Sting is above all polite, courteous. To say that is to seem somewhat condescending, but it is true that I had not expected a 'pop star' to be so gentlemanly. He offered me two tickets to hear him perform at Madison Square Garden, but the idea of getting mixed up with twelve hundred schoolgirls was too daunting. I thanked him but I didn't go. I would like to see him because I am convinced that there is something that he *is* on stage, over and above anything he *does*, for he has such a spellbinding effect on his audience. '. . . and then that wonderful voice', a woman concluded when speaking of him. I would have said that he had a singularly appealing, plaintive, untrained tenor voice. If you describe it as 'wonderful', what word have you left for Mr Pavarotti's singing? 'I think he is one of the best-looking guys around', a young man said to me. Again, without wishing in any way to diminish his greatness, I would have described him as tallish, slimmish, blondish, and with a very *aware* look in the eyes – as opposed to most stars who are self-regarding and do not look out of their faces but turn their eyes inward, like Hamlet's mother but without any of her feelings of misgiving as they contemplate their very souls. In this he was the direct opposite of Mr Warhol, who would turn his face towards you but never look at you, presenting his image to the world like a shield.

I used to try to stampede Mr Warhol into saying something because he had plenty to say, as is indicated by his book *From A to B and Back Again*, but I never could. If I went to a gathering of free-loaders, and standing apart from the others was a man approaching middle age, looking rather ill and saying nothing, that was Mr Warhol. He would say, when he became aware of your proximity, 'We must be photographed.' Those were the only words I ever heard him utter.

There is a whole book to be written about being the one among the many, the way in which your size and luminosity seem to increase as you become the focus of a crowd's attention, and the way in which the crowd sees something, some quality in you that you cannot name simply because you stand alone and above them. It is the lure certain professions carry with them – teaching, preaching, acting, politics. They are all vocations adopted by people who cannot live within their income of praise. The average man casts about for some poor benighted girl who can be persuaded to say, 'Oh, Rodney, you're ripping.' As soon as the words have been uttered he can get on with his life but there are other people who think to themselves, 'All right, *she* says it, but what about all those other people out there? They haven't said a thing.' And they become restless and television makes their fever worse because they can see two people in Patagonia who are talking about some other person and it drives them mad. So they lift themselves up until the whole world can see them. That is the function of the professions of teaching, preaching, acting and politics and it is why the people hungry for acknowledgement adopt them.

Mr Donne was wrong. It is not true that no man is an island. Except in America, every man is an island seeking to establish trade relations across a dark and dangerous sea. In the United States, everybody takes an interest in everybody else. Of course, though this is wonderful, it encourages gossip and everything has to be known about everybody. I can see that if an evangelist is a secret fornicator, this weakens his hold on morality, but if a politician is known to have had an affair with a typist in a past life, how can this possibly have anything to do with his capacity to rule the world? Nay, I will say more. Would you expect a man who has the energy, the imagination, the daring to think that he can rule the world to display some of these qualities in his private life? The answer seems to be No. America was founded by Puritans and this means that no one should set his sights on the White House until he is so old that all the typists he ever employed (in any capacity whatsoever) are dead.

Only acting is untroubled by this dilemma. An actress is expected to behave badly. Tallulah Bankhead's popularity lay in the fact that the English bourgeoisie went to see her to marvel that anyone so wicked could still move and speak. In America the critics panned her every performance but she transcended their notices. She had entered the profession of being to which we all aspire.

With all these considerations in mind, I have been into films. Firstly *The Bride* with Mr Sting. Then *Orlando*, in which I played Elizabeth I. It was the sort of picture that I would never have seen in a thousand years if I had not been in it. I would have termed *Orlando* unabashed festival material but I would have been wrong. It had a sporadic release all over America and, on the streets of the Lower East Side of Manhattan, I was compelled to cope with people walking backward before me, genuflecting and kissing my hand for several weeks after the film's release.

Being in a film is like giving birth. For a few hours after, while the memory of the suffering is clear in your mind, you swear you will never go through such an ordeal again, but when sufficient time has elapsed and the memory has faded, you have another baby or make another film. In the case of filming, it is the money that is the lure. For two weeks of suffering you are paid sufficient wages to live without doing anything in Manhattan for six months. What the lure of childbirth is I cannot imagine. I would have thought that the moment a woman discovers for certain that she is pregnant would be the worst time in her life. She knows she will not go to the movies for seventeen years.

The American people have done so much for me, have restored so fully my self-confidence, that I am constantly twisting and turning in an effort to live up to their expectations of me. Ingrid Bergman said, 'You must go on the stage knowing they want you to succeed.' She meant American audiences. In England the people in the stalls sit back in their chairs with folded arms, saying in their stony hearts, 'We've paid a hell of a lot for these seats. We hope you're going to DO something.' In Manhattan, the audience is leaning forward eagerly, crying, 'Tell us!' You can tell them anything – how to be beautiful, how to be successful, how to be thin, how to be saved. They will listen intently.

As a friend remarked, I decided to come to America at an age when most people decide to go into a nursing home. I wish I could have come here sooner when I had the energy and the optimism to fling myself with more abandonment, more total commitment, into all opportunities for self-promotion that are offered to me, but I couldn't pay my fare. When I say this people laugh nervously as though it were a joke, but it is the ugly truth. I never earned more than twelve pounds a week in my life in England. There it was enough. My old age was taken care of by Mrs Snatcher. When the day came when I could no longer see or hear or walk, she would spread her iron wings over me. But I would have been saving up for three years to spend three hours in Manhattan so I waited until I was invited by Mr Bennett, the darling of the Shubert Theaters, to visit Manhattan.

That is the story of my life: I go where my fare is paid. Because I have lived so long and travelled so far, I have passed from a masculine space to a feminine one but from a feminine time to a masculine era. I use these terms because gender is a preoccupation at this time and in this place. England is a masculine country. It appropriates and owns other countries. America endeavours (unsuccessfully) to soothe and appease other countries, which is a singularly feminine attitude. Nevertheless I have arrived here at a conspicuously masculine time. When I was young, there was a 'woman problem'. All novels were written by women for women about women. My mother read two of these books a week from W.H. Smith's lending library in Sloane Square. Their plots described discreetly but fervently a series of affairs in which the heroine indulged, but the authoress never forgave the heroine's husband for not understanding and appreciating his wife's 'inward and essential virginity'.

In other arts women also ruled. The words 'movie star' referred to women. Valentino was the only actor who could be called a movie star and he was a pseudo-woman. I am not impugning his sexual orientation in saying this but describing his image – withdrawn, mysterious, capricious. All other actors were in support of the female star and, in German films, any numbers of hours were spent on redeeming her appearance from a disfiguring naturalism while the men all looked dreadfully like human beings. Movies were made for a female audience. Now they are made for kids and the stars are men who spend their time smashing everything in sight, which is what all children want to do.

This shift in direction is particularly worrying to me. When I was young a homosexual man was thought to be effeminate. He dressed in women's clothes at every possible moment and adopted an exaggeratedly feminine gait like a model on a catwalk. This tradition has been brought to an abrupt end in America by 'political correctness'. The gay community, because it insists on being equal with real people, has decided that homosexual men are not an inferior race and so parade an egregious masculine image, wearing crew-cut hair, a kitchen tablecloth shirt, pre-ruined jeans, tractor boots and a small moustache, if not a full beard. They mate with other gargoyles of masculinity, scorning or regarding with pitying contempt those of us who cannot rise to such manliness. There is now no quasi-normal, masculine-feminine, satyr-nymph, pursuer-pursued courtship in the gay world – and, come to think of it, none in the real world either where women have decided to be people.

When I was writing *Manners From Heaven*, I read every book about etiquette and good manners that I could find. I was surprised to discover that all such compendia written before the Second World War devoted half their space to the question of how to comport yourself in the presence of 'the ladies'. Now there are no ladies. I mentioned this dearth on a television programme conducted by a female televisionary and she was affronted. 'I don't think we're putting up with that, are we, girls?' she asked of her audience. The girls said 'No'. I reminded them that they had decided to be people. 'Well, we are people,' they replied, still more affronted. I retreated in confusion. If they are people, they can open the damned door themselves.

Courtship happened because women were more precious as well as more frail than mere men. If the world is going to contain no women – only people – it will rapidly become faster, harsher, louder and the only subjects ever discussed will be sport, sex and money. Nevertheless, I have not gone into half-mourning, pending these unpleasant changes. I am laughing (behind my fan) because I shall have left before they are noticeable.

Every person of my age deplores the contemporary scene because deploring is a rich person's hobby. Writers are great deplorers and writers are always rich. They have the spare time to write. Indeed it is the plethora of hours that is their undoing. Poor Mr Wordsworth and Mr Tennyson wandered about the Lake District or sat in their town houses trying to find something – anything – to pontificate about and wrote a lot of rubbish because of this lack of urgency, this absence of engagement. Mr Hemingway and Mr Mailer scribble between other activities, which does nothing for their style but increases the excitement in their writings.

Those who are compelled to work do not deplore the changes that have come to modern life. They welcome fast transport, immediate communication, universal hygiene, modern medicine and the fact that now justice reaches into the smallest pockets of society. But I, who have not worked in many a long year, do not notice these improvements. I am concerned with the high gloss on society, not with its inner machinery. I am a free-loader, a dilettante, a butterfly on the wheel.

And that's putting it nicely.

QUENTIN CRISP
New York, Spring 1995

The Journals

1990

Spring

*

I can no longer indulge in orgies of sloth

I try not to be cultural. To this end, I have declined an invitation from an organization called *Operation Earth* to attend a gala celebration at the Hard Rock Café, although it was to take place at a cosy time in the evening instead of the middle of the night, and I was assured that I would not be asked to do or say anything. I might even have been given a drink and some funny things on sticks to eat. In short, this might have been a very pleasant evening on the peanut circuit, but I felt that for me to take advantage of this generous offer would be hypocritical in the extreme. I almost never watch programmes on the worthy Channel 13, I am totally uninterested in the fate of the sperm whale (what does it expect with a name like that?), and I regard the earth as a courageous global experiment that failed.

I rarely visit art galleries, for two reasons: the first is that there is never anywhere to sit, and the second is that I do not understand art. When people ask me what I've got against pictures, I can only reply, 'What have you got against the wall?'

The exhibition now at the Trabia Gallery is of works by a Mr la Chapelle. They are described as cibachromes. I have no idea what, technically, that word means, but visually they appear to be photographs that started as monochromes and were coloured later. This elevates them into the realm of art since, though photography may be an art, it can only be considered to be Art if the process of reproduction has been manipulated. How these pictures were accomplished is as interesting as what they mean, and, for once, we have here the right to consider their meaning because, in the catalogue, they have titles of a transcendental nature, such as 'The Search for Truth' and 'Victory Over Nature'. Ostensibly, the subject matter is the nude – most often male, and frequently in a state of conflagration like one of Mr Pryor's worst nightmares. However, in spite of their subject matter, none of these works is in the least pornographic.

The occasion seemed to be a success in the sense that the gallery was full to bursting, chiefly of men under the age of thirty-five dressed in black. (One of the guests explained to me that, below Houston Street, black is worn.) For once there were more people present than photographers. Everybody drank a lot of wine and talked animatedly to the people around him, but whether any pictures were sold I have no notion. Some of them cost more than $12,000. As I wandered out into the night, I couldn't help reflecting that I could live with abandonment on that sum for at least two years.

In *The Waste Land*, when Mr Eliot wrote that 'April is the cruellest month' he was thinking about his income taxes. I dealt with this annual problem last week, though my life in England did nothing to prepare me for the ordeal. In Britain, money is not taken very seriously, and banking is a cottage industry. When I lived there, if I darted into the Chelsea branch of Lloyds Bank and said to a teller, 'Is he in?', she would at once reply, 'I'll see.' In spite of my casual manner, she knew that I was referring to the manager; if he was not actually with a customer, he would deal with me at once. In the days when I was embroiled in the serpentine rituals of acquiring a passport, he trimmed my photographs down to the right size with his own penknife on his own desk.

In America I would not expect ever to stand in the august presence of a bank manager – nay, not even if I were a self-confessed millionaire. Here banks are solemn places the size of cathedrals, and they are manned by black ladies of such elegance that their ankles are no wider than other people's wrists. These beautiful creatures start to smile the moment they see me arriving because they know that I will have no idea what I am supposed to be doing. On one occasion I mentioned to one of them my bewilderment at finding that I had two accounts. 'That is correct,' she said. 'You do.' When I asked why, she replied in a sorrowful tone, 'I think you need an accountant.'

I have now acquired one. He is a gentleman of limitless patience who sits like a large hamster in a nest of papers. I have never actually seen him chew up the more troublesome documents and store them in his cheeks, but I suspect that is where they are. With the passing of the years, he has come to accept my invincible ignorance and even to condone it. Once, when I apologized to him for being more trouble than all his other victims put together, because of my stupidity in money matters, he replied, 'I don't understand them and I'm in the business.' What he does comprehend is that I place myself in his hands because I cannot fill in forms and not because I want my taxes to be diminished. I like my payments to the Internal Revenue Service to be large to show my loyalty to Mr Bush. I am only a resident alien and greatly fear the deportation that was forced upon the great gangsters when they defaulted on their taxes. 'Don't let them send me to Sicily,' I cry.

Having done my duty to the government, I hoped to enjoy many nights of peaceful sleep, but this was not to be. At about four o'clock one morning last week, I was awoken by my telephone bell. My totally unknown caller wanted to know if I had ever suffered from a venereal disease and whether I knew that Miss Garbo had died. I answered 'No' to the first question and 'Yes' to the second. The stranger then said with a wistful intonation, 'I suppose that means that we shall all die.'

It does.

Miss Garbo was so reclusive that it will be hard to guess if she enjoyed her later years, but, in the manner of her death, I would say that she was fortunate. Once, on-stage, when I was heaping praise on the fair name of Miss Crawford, a woman in the audience said, 'You think she was marvellous, but she died an alcoholic and alone.' I would have thought that was the ideal way to go. In old age, one of our preoccupations is how to die without violence and without pain. If we have the money to buy enough booze to deaden our senses, why not do so? Another problem arises if we expire in the presence of our friends. We have then to die and be polite at the same time. It may not be easy.

A Miss Mackenzie has presented me with a book of English crossword puzzles. I mustn't claim that they are better than those devised by other nations, but they are different in that solving them requires only ingenuity. American puzzles demand general knowledge which, as I barely live in the real world, I lack. I don't know the names of the capitals of obscure African countries; I don't know the first names of long-dead baseball players. Crossword puzzles are the aerobics of the soul. I become neurotic if I cannot complete my spiritual exercises for the day.

Nothing much has happened to me lately, except a few interviews conducted on the Mahomet Principle. That is to say that, since I decline to visit England, British journalists and photographers have to come to see me. The interviewers are lucky because, my room being at the back of the house, the roaring of the motorbikes belonging to the Hell's Angels cannot be heard. But photographers are in trouble. My living space is so small and so dark that they find themselves trampling backwards over heaps of dirty laundry or over piles of rejected typescripts to reach a spot from which more than the end of my nose comes into focus.

The number of invitations that I am able to accept is regrettably diminishing as I grow older. Some of these offer entertainment that I feel sure I would enjoy but which begins at half past ten. That is an hour at which I might still be awake, but I know that decorum forbids me to be found standing outside the doors when they open. When I was about six years old, my mother felt obliged to give a children's party; it was set to begin at three o'clock and precisely at that hour the front doorbell rang. My mother turned her head like a startled moorhen. 'Oh,' she screeched, 'who could be so ill-bred as to arrive at the right time?'

An unknown woman has telephoned me to ask if she might interview me. Removing my typewriter from my lap, I said, 'Interrogate me and I will reply.' Her first question was, 'Why is your number in the Manhattan directory?'

This is one of the great mysteries concerning which America and I remain for ever in postures of mutual amazement. What, I ask the world, is the use of a telephone if my number is unlisted? It means that no one will ever be able to call me; I will have to call him. Think of the expense. In fact, I hardly ever initiate a telephone conversation. I wait for the world to communicate with me. At least, this ensures that I am unlikely to be a nuisance to anybody.

My unknown interviewer then asked if I did not receive calls from a lot of weird people. I do, but, as I am the weirdest of them all, I can hardly complain. When, on one of his television programmes, Mr David Letterman first asked me this same question, it did instigate a lot of calls of a teasing nature and, during the next six months, about half a dozen threats upon my life. These I took calmly; I am accustomed to such treatment because, in England, I endured half a dozen such menaces a day. In America, after a while, the angry voices grew silent; nothing sinister happened until a few days ago. Then a girl called me and asked me to write on a piece of paper the words 'I love Tony', and to sign them; she proposed to come to the house where I live and collect it later in the day. I refused. Hours later, she called again, and again I said I would do no such thing. Then someone, posing as her boyfriend, called to say that if I didn't grant her request she would meet with some terrible fate. He said that he didn't know why I had been chosen for this hideous hoax.

A likely story! What can it all mean? Can any woman, however young, however carefully brought up, not know that she was trying to inveigle a self-evident gay man into signing a compromising statement? If she is innocent, who bribed, cajoled, or bullied her into such a murky situation?

Equally strange but in no way sinister was a letter I received from a gentleman living in Shreveport, Louisiana. He wants to collect drawings done of me by English art students. Perhaps he does not know how bad those efforts were. The British are not an artistic race; they go to art schools not to acquire skills in the arts but to avoid real life for a few adolescent years. My correspondent also asks if he can collect any of the book covers that I designed when I was a commercial artist some forty years ago, but these too are bad. I was forced into the arts as a way of earning a living because my appearance was so bizarre that it was totally unacceptable in the context of real work. I had no talent for anything.

The strangest part of this letter is a request for permission for a friend of his to perform the show I used to do in MacDougal Street in 1978. I am greatly flattered by all this interest in my past, and as far as I'm concerned his friend may don a blue wig, adopt an English accent, and quote me as saying anything, but there is no script; there never was. I went on to the stage and said what I thought. There are, of course, the possibilities of legal squabbles. A record of the show as done in the Village was made by a Mr Fordin and videotape produced by a firm called, of all things, Family Home Entertainment. I have no idea whether or not either of these companies would say they had rights that had been infringed. I wouldn't like to be dragged into court. What would I wear?

I have entered into the Avenue C life.

It all began with an invitation to a play by Eric Bentley. Now, as is well known, I do not hold with the theatre. For one thing, it is subject to error: at every moment on-stage something could go wrong. In the movies, by contrast, nothing goes wrong; everything is perfect. Even a bad movie is perfectly bad. For another thing, by comparison with the movies, the stage is as intimate as a football field. Our vision of a play is telescopic. We can hardly tell whether the leading lady is smiling or frowning. This handicap seduces her into multiplying her every gesture, her every word by the seating capacity of the theatre. She embraces us with semaphore gestures and tells us her secrets in the voice of a town crier while we, anxious to communicate our appreciation, clap and cheer out of all proportion to the price of the seat we have been given.

Nevertheless, I did not feel that I could decline this invitation to Professor Bentley's play. I know the professor; I once worked for him in a play entitled *Lord Alfred's Lover*. In that production I did not take my part very seriously because, at the time, I had not been told about the author's greatness. Since then, my education in this matter has been completed by a visit to a huge lecture hall on 128th Street. There the crowned heads of American literature were gathered together to honour Professor Bentley. I was frightened because I already had some inkling of how highbrow the atmosphere would be. I had received a book full of articles about him or on subjects that it was thought would interest him. I was asked to write some phrases that would enhance the value of this impressive tome, but had evaded this request on the ground that, at this exalted level of culture, praise from me would do more damage than other people's blame. Nevertheless, I attended the party for the sake of the peanuts. It was a most enlightening occasion.

It transpired that Professor Bentley is unique, and unique in many ways: he is a cabaret artiste, a drama critic, a translator, and a dramatist. His appearance is traditional; he is tall, thin, grey-haired, but to say that his manner is unexpectedly human is not enough. He is skittish. His latest play is called *German Requiem* and is what Mr Goldwyn would have described as 'freely adapted' from a work by Mr Heinrich von Kleist. Its theme is a Romeo and Juliet tale of two young lovers from hostile dynasties. It is Plantagenet in appearance, but Jacobean in style; that is to say that, by the end of it, hardly anybody is still living and those who are regret it.

This tragedy is now playing at The Living Theater, which is situated on my street but at the edge of the world. It ought to be called The Hardly Living Theater. As you look round the foyer, you feel certain it was once a shoe-repair shop. The acting space is depressingly small, but no one could deny that it has been utilized with quite astonishing ingenuity. Because there is no stage and no curtain, the various scenes (and there are many) are acted in different parts of the theatre, including halfway up one wall. As I have noticed in all such cramped and impoverished circumstances, quite inexplicably the lighting equipment is as elaborate as that of any Broadway theatre and was expertly controlled.

In spite of being totally out of my depth in such a rarefied atmosphere, I enjoyed the play. Before it began, I asked the Professor if I would understand it. His reply was, 'Only too well.' He was right. It echoes in more sonorous language than I can command my deepest convictions. I once met Mr William Burroughs. Within minutes of our being introduced, he said, 'What is worth having is worth fighting for,' and I replied, 'That which we can only maintain by force we should try to do without.'

That is what *German Requiem* is all about.

People keep asking me what I do when I'm not on television. As, even in a good year, I have never been on television more than four times, and as many interviews last less than five minutes, there is a lot of time for which to account. Obviously I must give a very long or very superficial answer. I feel more at ease with the second kind of response. 'I do what you do,' I reply, 'when you're not on television.' These words frighten some people; they blush or gasp, 'What's that?' I tell them that I wash socks, file my nails, write my letters, and fry an egg. What I refrain from mentioning is that much of the time is spent dozing.

They say that camels store water in their humps so as to be able to make long journeys across deserts without suffering acute thirst. I have never sunk so low as to drink water, but in other respects I used to be like the camel. If I foresaw that I was unlikely to be able to cadge a square meal from anybody for some time, I would immediately eat everything in sight. Similarly, if it did not seem that I would have a good night's sleep for the next forty-eight hours, I would at once go to bed and will myself into unconsciousness for as long as I could. Now that I am old, I find that I can no longer indulge in the orgies of sloth. I sleep more superficially and for shorter periods of time spread over any twenty-four-hour period. To avoid waking at dawn (never one of my favourite times of day), I retire later and later. This habit has tempted me into watching films on late-night television. I know this is a mortal sin and I have mentioned my sleep problem at some length in the hope of explaining, if not excusing, this reprehensible behaviour.

Most nocturnal re-runs are of unsuccessful movies trying to recoup their losses from hapless insomniacs. Many of them are about creatures from outer space, mad scientists, and haunted houses, but some are very immediate and very real. One such picture which I saw quite recently was entitled *Our Family Honour*. I enjoyed it enormously, but it raised the age-old, disturbing question about the pernicious influence of films upon their audiences.

I do not hold that any movie, however valid, can reverse a person's natural inclinations. For instance, I do not think that if *Scenes from the Class Struggle in Beverly Hills* were shown in a convent, all the inmates would instantly become sex maniacs. However, I do think that a well-made film can endorse and even appear to justify opinions that are already waiting for some corroboration. In this way, a movie like *Our Family Honour* can be dangerous. It is a fast-moving, vividly photographed, and well-acted story of the battle between the police family who want their father to be made commissioner and a Mafia-type organization headed by the wonderful Mr Eli Wallach. The cops finally triumph, but by brutal means of which the director appears to approve. The police are seen laying waste entire bars and pool halls. There seems to be no difference between their tactics of intimidation and those of the baddies. We all fear the police, and wisely. As the head of Scotland Yard once said, 'If a policeman is popular, there is something wrong.' In a world where another cop is killed almost every week, is it not a bad thing for a picture like *Our Family Honour* to justify our learning not to respect but to hate the police?

I put this notion forward in the form of a question, fearing that a direct statement might make me into that least accommodating of all geometrical figures – a kinky square.

When not watching films in the dead of night, I am occasionally asked to take part in one by day. I do not know why this happens, because I am not an actor, have received no theatrical training, and am always slightly embarrassed by being asked to utter other people's words. In spite of this considerable drawback, there is in existence a film of *Hamlet* in which I speak some of Mr Polonius's lines. The press said that I 'gave an unusual rendering'. That was putting it kindly. The picture was made by a Mr Coronado in the Royal College of Art, and was intended to win him a degree.

Much of the same kind of situation seems to prevail here in New York University, with one curious difference. All films made by American students or people on the amateur fringe of the movie industry have supernatural or allegorical themes: all are at some remove from reality. I have never dared to ask why; I have merely obeyed instructions. This endeavour to avoid saying no to anything has led me into presiding at a feast of freaks under Brooklyn Bridge, to sitting at the head of the boardroom table of some secret society and even to standing beside an actress called Miss Bolger on the roof of a house on Ludlow Street with our toes sticking out over the edge (Miss Gish was never more dedicated than that).

Now I have been offered another such part by a more established director. In order that I may know what is involved in this project, he has lent me a book of stories by a Mr McGrath on the first of which the film will be based. As I find that this project would oblige me to take off all my clothes, I think it is very unlikely that I shall accept the role, but my meeting with the director was by no means in vain. He gave me lunch, and the book, called *Blood and Water and Other Stories*, has given me hours of pleasure. The author is described as 'The Poe of the '80s', but he is more than that, because a sexual element, absent from the work of the master, has seeped into these tales. Other Gothic writers seek to haunt their readers. Mr McGrath wishes to disgust us; he describes the physical and psychological oddities with such evident relish that they become hilarious. His characters and the situations in which he depicts them are like Charles Addams illustrations commissioned by Grove Press. I would recommend this book to anyone who longs for a glimpse of something worse than real life.

Summer

*

*It would be less depressing to be alcoholic than
to be anonymous*

In a movie entitled *Ace in the Hole*, Mr Kirk Douglas said, 'Good news is no news.' Working on this principle, whenever television has deigned to show us aerial pictures of Ohio, the entire state has been flooded. We have seen pets fished out of muddy pools, children being taken to school in boats, and cars with their headlights just above the water level glaring at us like the eyes of alligators.

I have now been to Dayton and am happy to be able to allay anyone's fears. It is a bone-dry, quiet, spacious city full of the friendliest people. Having been invited there to speak at a Gay Pride festival, I was astonished to discover that Dayton has at least four hundred gay people, all of whom turned up to hear me cheer them on. I was asked by a member of my audience how Dayton compared with New York. I said that it is cosier. I hope that was the correct answer; I noticed a veiled apprehension among Daytonians that a stranger might evince a trace of condescension towards their home town. One young man said, 'You've been to Iowa. We're practically a suburb of Manhattan compared with them.'

When arriving in Dayton, the first surprise is the airport. Though not as vast as the one in Atlanta, it is large and brand-new. In the entrance there is a piece of gleaming metal sculpture symbolizing world air travel. I am so ignorant that, until my hosts enlightened me, I did not know that Dayton is the birthplace of aviation. Later, to reinforce this point, they took me to see the home of the Wright brothers, an impressive Tara-style mansion on the top of a hill. I stayed comfortably in the home of the organizers of the Gay Pride festivities and, on my first evening there, they gave a small party.

The following evening was a much grander affair than I had expected. Five long tables had been set up for dinner with vases of flowers and balloons in a vast gymnasium. On an upper floor were several tables loaded with hors d'œuvres between trays of brightly coloured condoms; it was possible to mistake them for toffee wrappers. I did not avail myself of any safeguards against contamination, but I ate salmon and signed books supplied by a local gay bookshop. By this time, I was wearing not only a rose given to me by my hosts from their garden, but also an orchid so large that later, when I spoke, wisps of maidenhair fern trembled under my chin.

On the main floor there was a small stage where entertainment was provided first by a female solo singer and later by a men's choir, who sang some of Mr Porter's lyrics. Inevitably, this made 'I Get A Kick Out Of You' sound somewhat like an anthem, but it was all very enjoyable. The main part of the evening's activities was taken up with speeches. These were about gay pride and were of a very self-congratulatory nature, but justifiably so. In spite of the fact that no alcohol was served during the entire evening, a truly joyful, friendly atmosphere prevailed. It was a well-organized event attended by nearly four hundred men and women, all presumably gay, or what a politician would call 'fellow travellers'.

Whoever would have thought there was so much happy sin in Ohio?

I returned to Manhattan with just enough time to change my socks before setting out for Tampa, where I had been summoned for much the same reason as I had been summoned to Dayton: to tell serried ranks of gay people that they must be brave. Here, though, the audience was very different – everyone was dressed in a three-piece suit – and the city was very different. As with every other city in Florida that I have seen, the general impression is one of boundless luxury (beginning with the apartment I was allowed to occupy in the absence of its two owners). My host was a lawyer most of whose clients are homosexual. Since so many gay couples start nesting within minutes of exchanging telephone numbers, he must be perpetually busy with property disputes, but for the three days of my visit justice slept, magistrates played golf, and law courts were empty while he very kindly showed me the many fascinating features of the city. I was amazed to learn what a huge business the making of cigars had once been in Tampa – an industry now kept alive almost single-handedly by George Burns.

When I expressed my awe at the splendours of Tampa, its perpetual sunshine, its wide, white streets, its bay in which the sea creeps humbly towards the expensive shore, a young woman tried to disillusion me. 'Tampa,' she said, 'is like a little girl tottering about in her mother's high-heeled shoes and pretending that she is grown-up and sophisticated.' I was surprised by this judgement; only the friendliness of everybody that I met had prevented me from feeling totally outclassed.

On the first evening, I was taken to a party at a house where we ate in a garden that ran down to the water's edge. The only hint of rowdiness occurred when the owner of the house pushed the gentleman who had driven us to the party (in a Rolls-Royce, no less) into the swimming pool. As the victim of this prank was the nicest possible man who had neither said nor done anything out of place, no one was amused by the incident; in fact, they were frightened by it and ran, squeaking, from the pool's edge, fearing that they might suffer a similar fate. I tried to remain calm, but I was bewildered. I know the rich are heartless, but this gesture seemed positively Roman in its contempt for human feelings.

I may have spoken toon soon. In a recent entry in this journal, I said that I had found Dayton to be bone-dry. I still hope it is, but I have now learned that, the very moment I left Ohio, almost the entire state was flooded again. *Après moi le déluge.*

*   *   *

I have now made eight flights in one month. Since going to Dayton and Tampa, I have visited Houston and Chicago. I trust that none of these fair cities will now be attacked by tornados.

I was sent to Houston a long time ago to speak to all the redeemed heavy drinkers in Texas. I did my best to utter words of comfort, but was by no means sure of my ground. Secretly I have always held the opinion that it would be less depressing to be alcoholic than to be anonymous.

Last Tuesday, with once again only time to change my socks, I went to Chicago, a city even more familiar to me than Houston because I once worked in its Ivanhoe Theater for a whole month. The high point of that earlier visit was an appearance on television co-starred with (well, seated next to) Mr T., the mountainous, muscle-bound star of television's 'The A Team'. And he truly is a star. He is so vast that I was obliged to ride him side-saddle. Though he was clanking with precious metal and bristling with diamonds, as he lowered himself majestically into a creaking chair, his first words were, 'I am a very humble man.'

On this more recent visit, I did not appear on television, but was interviewed several times on radio programmes. One of these was conducted by Mr Terkel; I had known that it would be. The first law of Chicago is that no one can enter or leave without accounting for himself to Studs Terkel. He was in his usual benign form and seemed to be able to remember every meeting we have ever held.

When not caught up in this frenzy of conviviality, I stayed in the Belmont Hotel, from the roof garden of which I could see almost the entire city. It stretched to the uttermost horizon in all directions, and the lake, of which we had a magnificent view, assumed the airs and graces of an ocean; even from the thirteenth floor, it was impossible to see the other side, and its waves crashed against a long, sandy shoreline teeming with sunbathers and even real bathers. It certainly puts the Lake District of England in its place. It also seemed to ventilate the city, which was as hot as New York but nothing like as oppressive.

Having made so many journeys by air and visited four different states in one month, it has taken me quite a while to slow down. Just as a sprinter, having broken the tape, runs on for several yards, so for about four days after my return from Chicago I did everything fast and with lunatic intensity.

The first task against which I have flung myself was answering the mail. I threw away a heap of invitations to events that had already come and gone while I was away; I tore up all requests for money (you wouldn't think that anyone whose address is East Third Street would ever receive begging letters, but they do); then I started on the more personal demands. The oddest of these came from an unknown woman living in the middle of England asking for a lock of my hair. I thanked her for her interest in my unworthy self, but I did not pander to her kinkiness. At my age, I haven't so much hair left that I can afford to distribute any among strangers. Lastly, I turned my attention to dealing with news of the dead. This is reaching harrowing proportions because, in middle age in a frantic effort to seem young, I associated chiefly with people older than I. One such person was a famous theatrical photographer called Angus McBean.

When I first met him, the Second World War had just begun. I was thirty and he was thirty-four. When he told me his age, I tried to keep my face absolutely still. I did not want to evince the least tremor of surprise, but secretly I had thought that he was about fifty. He was tall, painfully thin, bearded, and bald. Furthermore, as he himself once remarked, all the lines in his face went 'the wrong way'. I don't think that any of these defects mattered in the least to his innumerable friends, but they did to him, because he was obsessed with the notion of physical beauty. He was lucky in that he was then living in a happier time when all photographic negatives were glass and could be retouched outrageously. He – or, rather, his retoucher – even transformed Edith Evans into a great beauty.

Mr McBean retouched not only the portraits that he took, but also the houses he lived in, and there were many. He caused the doors in one of his homes to be painted to look as though they were open when in fact they were shut; ceilings were decorated to appear like beams festooned with grape vines; alcoves seemed like apertures through which the next room was visible. It would not be an exaggeration to say that he retouched his whole life. The tragic result of this wall-to-wall fantasy was that he never saw the danger he was in. When, after about a year of silence, the war began to shake London to its foundations, he moved to Bath. There, his exotic lifestyle became instantly conspicuous, and soon met with disapproval. The police broke into his house in which he had generously allowed various young men to take refuge from the bombardment of the capital. Though the youngest of the boys was living there at his mother's request, Mr McBean was charged with the perversion of minors, found guilty, and jailed for four years.

While he was 'away', his mother lived in the lodge of a large country house in Somerset where my mother was a guest. Because the lodge possessed no telephone, it was at the big house that a call from 'Angus' arrived. My mother fetched Mrs McBean and, when the telephone conversation was over, asked her if she were Mrs McBean. Seeing that the poor lady was terrified by this question, my mother added, 'You have nothing to fear because I am Quentin Crisp's mother.' They instantly pooled their disgrace and became friends.

Upon being released Mr McBean courageously went on with his life as though nothing unpleasant had happened. In spite of his misfortune, in one respect he was lucky. He worked chiefly among stage people and they rallied round him. Actresses love a gesture. He became so famous that all his early negatives now lie in the archives at Harvard (or, possibly, Yale), but I doubt that he ever became rich. He spent his money on buying large houses, altering them, sometimes to the extent of removing whole walls or ceilings, selling them, and buying even bigger premises. The last time I ever visited him, he was living in East Anglia in a Tudor mansion surrounded by a moat. I started to laugh the very moment this vast edifice came into view. While I was staying there, Mr McBean was threatening to write his life story. I wonder if that document exists; it would be well worth reading.

Now that the fever of attending to my correspondence has passed, I have returned to being my customary, slothful self. The first thing that I noticed as I resumed my meandering course through the Lower East Side of Manhattan is how dilapidated New York seems after the newness of other cities – especially Houston. There the streets are wide, straight, smooth, and absolutely free of litter, and the buildings all look as though they were erected yesterday. Manhattan, by contrast, is beginning to acquire an Old World charm. It won't be long before Grand Central Station looks like the Parthenon.

When I'm away from home, I seldom watch television. When not engaged in the smiling and nodding racket, I sleep. By the time I returned to East Third Street, I had fallen out of the television habit. Several days passed without my staring at a single frame. When, finally, I succumbed to my old sinful ways, I was so out of practice that I mistook a play for a news event. In the rather fuzzy distance, I could see some men running along a wharf while an announcer's voice told me that several people had been shot. Knowing how passionately TV loves disaster, I took this information calmly. When some advertisements interrupted this scene, my suspicions were aroused, but only slightly. I honestly cannot predict whether, when the end of the world is announced, the information will be punctuated by the words, 'Closing Down Sale. Hurry! Hurry!' I only knew for certain that what I was watching was fiction when, on being told that one of their victims had died, the terrorists displayed feelings of remorse. Zealots are totally incapable of any emotion other than rage. It is an unalterable law that people who claim to care about the human race are utterly indifferent to the sufferings of individuals.

Autumn

*

*Local cockroaches are having the next-door
house remodelled*

Mrs Thatcher has abdicated; her acid reign is over. I shall spend
my final years in perpetual mourning – rather like Queen Victoria.

Mrs Thatcher ascended the throne during one of my early,
exploratory stage appearances in America. At that time, hardly an
evening passed without someone asking my opinion of England's
Prime Minister. I thought and still think that she was a star and
I repeatedly said so. Once, after a show, while a female member
of the audience was walking along the street with me, she said, 'I
hope you realize that you gave all the wrong answers.' When my
humble apologies finally subsided, she added, 'You are supposed
to be against Mrs Thatcher.' I was obviously expected to take
politics seriously; I never have.

Of course, if I had been born in China, Russia, or Cuba, I would
have been shot. Then, as I stood before the line of rifles, I would
have said, 'Hold your fire: I want to vote.' In Britain, going to the
polls is a waste of time. There are really only two factions: the Tories
and the Labourites, and whichever is in power, it doesn't take long
for people to start moaning, 'What went wrong with the Labour
(or Conservative) party?' It came to power: that's what went
wrong. The question is as pointless as asking what went wrong
with our marriage. We got married: that's what went wrong.

Politics are not an instrument for effecting social change; they
are the art of making the inevitable appear to be a matter of wise
human choice. Politics are not for people; they are for politicians
– a medium in which a person can suspend his monstrous ego. In

this respect, they fulfil exactly the same function as the stage or evangelism does for actors or preachers. The only benefit that can be derived by ordinary mortals from any of these vocations is that they present us with someone on whom we can focus our attention – even our passions – at least in a manner less fatuous than soccer. It is this human need that Mr Disraeli, Mr Lloyd George, Mr Churchill and Mrs Thatcher fulfilled so well. At first the world, and particularly the British press, tried to treat the last of these public figures as a joke or as a woman – which, in England, is much the same thing. One paper wrote, 'Mrs Thatcher arrived at the House of Commons looking dramatic in black.' These were not really words of praise, they were a cue for readers to regard her as frivolous. No one had ever said, 'Mr Wilson arrived looking commonplace in navy blue.' When the Falkland Islands suddenly loomed out of the Atlantic Ocean, the public, which had never before heard of the place, was forced to change its mind about the Iron Lady. She was the first politician in a very long time who did not try to rule the world and be loved at the same time.

For this, she has to be admired.

On Thanksgiving Day, as I have done for many years, I went again to Port Monmouth, New Jersey, where the parents of a friend of mine always welcome me. I regard this as a very special favour. Such occasions tend to be purely family affairs, and I am an outsider in so many ways. I doubt that any such thing would happen in England, but it is difficult to judge. There is no Thanksgiving Day on the British calendar. What have the English to be thankful for? In England, the eating of turkey is almost entirely confined to Christmas time; a turkey sandwich, which on the menus of New York delicatessens is a perennial item, would be regarded by Londoners as almost a blasphemy. Furthermore, apart from the differences in the history of the two nations, now that I have lived in America for many years I cannot help thinking of the southern English as a not particularly hospitable race. Of course, when I lived there, I acquired friends and they were very generous to me, but in general, public holidays and feast days, which encourage Americans to turn their attention outward towards acquaintances and even strangers, seem to cause British families to close ranks.

I have now seen Mr Attenborough's epic, *Gandhi*. I did not see this picture when it was first released on account of my deep-rooted aversion to British movies. Apparently, it won every possible award except one for costume design, presumably because sheets have only to be arranged rather than tailored. It fully deserves the praise lavished upon it. As an undertaking, it is formidable; its control of crowds is equal to that in *Gone With The Wind*, and Mr Kingsley is much more suitably cast as Mr Gandhi than Miss Leigh was in the role of Scarlett O'Hara. As a film, I did not think *Gandhi* was wholly a success, but I say this with bowed head because I know that, if I find fault with anything, I ought to be able to suggest what should have been done instead. In this instance, I can't. I can only say that, shortly after the massacre, *Gandhi* ceased to be a movie and became a documentary film. Though, very cleverly, the narrative begins with his assassination, we are not continuously drawn forward at an ever-increasing pace throughout the rest of the picture towards this climax. It is only during the final four or five minutes that our pulse quickens and, even then, we do not know why he was killed; we were never made aware of what specific danger he was in nor from what quarter disaster would spring.

It would have amounted to a kind of blasphemy to have mentioned it the other night, but, secretly, I could not repress the memory of a day when, some sixty years ago, English newspapers announced in bold letters that Mr Gandhi would 'fast unto death' if it would secure India her freedom. I overheard someone, who was surveying this announcement, say, 'It's the "unto" that will do the trick.'

*   *   *

I've now reached the age when almost every letter that I receive from anyone that I used to know in Britain contains a list of acquaintances who have recently died, and I have secretly wondered if this was ever going to pay off. Last week I thought it had. I received notification that I had been left two hundred pounds in somebody's will. As, with feverish fingers, I turned the pages of this document, my hopes began to fade. In order to get my hands on this legacy, I would have to sign for it, and my signature would have to be witnessed by a banker, a clergyman, or a justice of the peace who knows me personally. Where in the whole wide world will I find anyone with any prestige to lose who would admit to anything so incriminating?

So as to wring from anyone who may read this journal the last drops of sympathy, I will add that local cockroaches are having the next-door house remodelled and have temporarily moved into our house with their children. They sleep in my bed, eat the food from my plate, and even read the typescripts lying in a heap in one corner of my room.

In Mr Jonathan Nossiter's movie, *Resident Alien*, which is about me and New York City, Mr Michael Musto is shown saying, as if he were a dope pedlar, that he is in the business of handing out to the publicity addicts that infest this city their daily fix of fame without which they tend to become so restless. Last week, a Mr Duckett and a Mr Alig invited us to a positive orgy of notoriety: we celebrated Mr Musto's birthday at Limelight, the profane church on Sixth Avenue. As always, the music was too loud, but for the first time since the place was opened, it was lit so that we could actually see one another. We sat on real chairs at real tables and ate real food while from the stage Mr Musto introduced us to the lady who is the star of those television commercials that advertise the science-fiction gadget that helps put the helpless in instant communication with the Emergency Medical Service. She uttered into the microphone the by-now-famous line, 'I've fallen and I can't get up,' and was presented with the first Fallen Woman

Award. While we all applauded ecstatically, the girl sitting next to me murmured, 'That phrase is the story of my life.'

The guests wore clothes that ran the gamut from near nakedness, through every aspect of outrage, to deliberate dowdiness. It was quite impossible to distinguish them from the staff either by their appearance or their behaviour, since the waiters frequently kissed the diners whom they were serving. Naturally, Mr Musto looked more conspicuous than anybody else. He wore a silver topcoat over a green suit with large white stars, kinky fur shoes as big as canoes, and, of course, impenetrable dark glasses, and he embraced everyone. He really is the ideal host for such an occasion – never for a moment ceasing not merely to enjoy himself but also to be seen to do so.

During the evening, everybody photographed everybody, which prompted me to suggest that what is now needed is a periodical called *The Freeloader's Gazette*. Within minutes of my uttering these words, someone slapped on to our table a pile of magazines; I think they were actually entitled *Clubland*, but they obviously fulfilled exactly the same function as my proposed paper would do. Everybody who could reach a copy fast enough grabbed one and, at once, there was a hubbub like the noise in the parrot house at a zoo. 'Oh look,' they squawked, 'there I am and there's Tilly or Lilly or Billy or Willy.'

Whenever I make a feeble attempt to understand the financial basis on which such events are built, the glib response is always, 'It's all publicity.' I feign acceptance of this explanation, but secretly I harbour misgivings. If 'society' pictures and the accompanying gossip are only seen and read by the people featured in them, who never pay for anything, then who makes a profit, or, to pose a gloomier question, why is no one ruined by the staggering expense of it all?

When people ask me what I do when I am not involved in the smiling and nodding racket, I used to say, 'I breathe and I blink.' To these deliberately minimal activities, I must now add that I scratch. I suffer from eczema, which increases in severity with the passing years. Mr Eliot wrote that it is 'love that weaves the intolerable shirt of flame', but I'm wearing it, and I think it's eczema. Once, trying to elicit sympathy from an acquaintance, I asked him what he thought might be the cause of this strange malady. Without a moment's hesitation, he attributed it to the atmosphere in New York, and added, 'It's brought the Brooklyn Bridge to its knees and is tearing the façades from public buildings, why should it spare yours?'

Winter

*

I hate snow

Since I took up residence in the United States, so many kind people, some of them total strangers, have sent me gifts and greetings that I have come to feel acutely the lack of some easy means of expressing my gratitude to everybody in the world. Now, at last, it is to hand.

Merry Christmas, everybody!

Many who know me well may be surprised at this unaccustomed boisterousness, but, although my name has been mentioned in at least two books written by, for, and about curmudgeons, I am not really misanthropic. I merely do not have an aptitude for festivity – especially foreordained festivity – because I am by nature relaxed and happy. In the same way, I do not look forward with any special eagerness to annual holidays because, for some years past, my life has been one long vacation. Furthermore, I do not look well in a paper hat and am hopeless at what, in a time gone by, used to be called parlour games.

These are not inadequacies that have overtaken me in old age. Christmas has always been a period of acute embarrassment for me. What made the situation so absurd was the fact that, in spite of the generosity of Mr Claus, my mother used to give me two shillings so that I could buy a present for my father, and he gave me a similar sum to purchase something for my mother. On the appointed day, they both thanked me. Whom did they think they were kidding? Wishing to spare myself and my friends any reminder of such humiliating events, I have now abandoned as many rituals of the Yuletide season as possible; I try to carry on as though nothing unpleasant had happened, but, in England, it was necessary to be nice to somebody to get a square meal. Over there, the Christmas holidays may last for nearly a week. They have invented something called Boxing Day; this is the 26th of December and, in olden days, was when the dustmen, the postmen, and other public servants came knocking on the front door of the rich with money boxes and stood on the front doormat, wishing the owner a Merry Christmas until they were given a reward. If either the 25th or the 26th of December falls on a Saturday or Sunday, which for the most part are already days of rest, they feel cheated unless they are accorded some other day of idleness. During all that time England, never exactly a hardworking country, is shut. In these difficult circumstances, I have found it wise to fling myself upon the hospitality of a household where there are no children. This not only saves money, but also obviates having to crawl about on the floor, squeaking with delighted surprise, and other such humiliations.

But I have a message of hope to offer. If you ignore Christmas and all its attendant rituals, you have only about four years of disgrace to endure. If at the end of that time, anyone is still sending you a card or inviting you to a party, you can assume that his love is not merely a reflex reaction to convention, but is genuine and eternal and that, though he may expect gratitude, he will not demand from you a display of excessive merriment.

Being a sworn enemy of music – because it is the most noise conveying the least information – I have been to only one concert in my entire life, and that was many years ago and in another country. But I know Jack Eric Williams, who is a composer, a performer, and a teacher of music, and he is making continual efforts to effect a truce between me and culture. With this in view, he took me to an event infinitely more *recherché* than a mere concert – a *soirée musicale*. At least, that is what I took the occasion to be.

It occurred in the home of a Mr O'Horgan, who directed *Hair* and *Jesus Christ Superstar*, and who, on this particular evening, was a most agreeable host to about thirty people of all ages, from ninety down to a barefooted child, and of all sexes. We were assembled to hear a cantata entitled *The Child*, composed and conducted by a Mr Johnson. The singers included five or six excruciatingly fragile boys who are members of The Boys' Choir of Harlem. My ignorance prevents me from telling you if they sang well, but I can confidently assert that they behaved with the utmost decorum, considering the temptation to do otherwise. I am also unable to express any opinion of the music they performed, but the cantata was by no means the most astonishing aspect of the evening. Mr O'Horgan believes in music to an extent that I would not have thought possible. His apartment is dazzling. It is full, not of what might be called furniture, but of musical instruments. Apart from the grand piano used on this occasion, it contained another, much smaller keyboard instrument, three harps, and a huge drum. As if this did not display sufficient dedication to the Muse, the walls were encrusted with tambourines, rattles, and other devices whose function was too arcane for me to guess. Of course, this did little to make me like music any better, but it did make Mr O'Horgan the focus of my deepest interest – almost of reverence.

It is rapidly becoming a tradition that when a friend of mine, who has gone to teach in Kansas City, returns to New York for a breath of fresh happiness, we go to the theatre. Because his subject is what used to be known as elocution, we tend to choose a British play in which there is an emphasis on words rather than deeds. I think this is an aspect of the national character. In England, people over the age of thirty seem to care what they say and how they say it because their accent is a clue to class, which is so important to them. Here, there is no class and, in any case, speech has gone out of fashion. Music speaks louder than words, and in all public places, it is raised to such a volume that only a trained orator could make himself heard.

Our last visit to a theatre was to see *Lettice and Lovage*, which is a torrent of words. This time we chose *Shadowlands*. This is a play about C.S. Lewis, who wrote fantastic stories for children with one hand, and with the other, dissertations on the Anglo-Catholic religion. He was also a university teacher. This profession ideally suited him to be the central character in a drama about abstruse ideas expressed in languages festooned like a Christmas tree with glittering metaphors and similes. Indeed, *Shadowlands* begins with the hero delivering a lecture to the audience in which he tries to explain why God has made life so horrible. Though Americans mistrust words – especially unfamiliar ones – their reverence for the theatre is so great that they remained calm.

As the story unfolds, its participants are drawn at a dignified pace from the serenity of English university life into the turgid real world, from happy celibacy through awkward marriage to widowerhood, and all the while, the God of the Christians has to be appeased. It was very embarrassing, but it was never dull.

The supporting cast is good. In a sense, their task is easy because, being English, they are acting the avoidance of reaction. When Jack Lewis informs his brother that he is getting married, the reply, after a pause, is, 'You surprise me.' Miss Alexander, whom we last saw on television in *Malice in Wonderland*, plays the Eve in this academic Eden, and she is wonderful. As we sat only three rows from the stage, I cannot judge how her performance 'reads' from a distance, but to us every word was audible and every glance was loaded with meaning.

The play's fundamental problem rests on the shoulders of a Mr Hawthorne, and he carries it commendably, even heroically. His only handicap is that he has to act charm; he does not possess any by nature. Charm has little to do with being handsome; it lies in a subtle willingness to please without grovelling, combined with the ability to make decisions without a hint of tyranny.

In my lifetime, the one facet of theatre that has changed more than any other is décor. It used to be called scenery, and its only function was to suggest convincingly a place and a time of day.

When I was young and thought that going to the theatre would make me seem to be an aesthete, most drama, other than the classics, was domestic and was played in front of what that formidable iconoclast, Joan Littlewood, called 'those bloody French windows'. All that is now ended.

Being in hiding from Mr Claus, I have only attended one other public event: a party for my eighty-second birthday (billed as my eighty-first – to cheer me up?). It took place at El Morocco. I have been there once before and thought I must wear nothing but black and white if I was to seem accustomed to its zebra motif, but in fact, the festivities occurred in a bright red upper room that looked like one of the chambers in Mr Poe's 'Masque of the Red Death'.

Our hostess was the Countess Erme Klent-de-Boen, and she very graciously did the whole routine, standing by the door for about an hour to welcome each new arrival. I was deeply impressed. The guests (hardly any of whom I knew except Jack Eric Williams) arrived in droves, but hardly any of them spoke to me. Contrary to custom at such functions, photographers were few, but just as I was leaving, a gentleman who seems pleased to be known as Ugly George appeared from the nearby twitching area, wearing only a few wisps of silvered leather and carrying on his shoulder a video camera. For a few seconds, co-starred with Mr Baird Jones, I smiled and said I was delighted to be there. Then I was permitted to depart.

An English poet, probably Thomas Hardy, describes actors as 'that sad, happy race'. Translated into prose, the phrase means 'that heart-rendingly optimistic bunch of misfits'. I can think of no other profession whose members are willing to take so much trouble to create anything so short-lived – except cooks who prepare elaborate feasts decorated with all sorts of visual effects, only to have their work demolished in minutes by a horde of unheeding locusts.

*   *   *

It has been snowing. I hate snow, and will never understand the people who persistently exclaim that it looks pretty. This is like being glad to be attacked by a handsome mugger. Snow is, at best, tiring to negotiate; at worst it is dangerously slippery and causes one to arrive in other people's houses and sit around for hours in wet socks.

I shall try to stay in my room until the spring. This plan involves a lot of two particular activities. One of these is watching television. When I lived in England, all good programmes came from the United States. If the participants were running fast and shooting straight, the drama was American. In those days, in Britain, only two channels existed, BBC or dog food: culture or entertainment. There was no room for all these quizzes, competitions, panels, games, and above all there were fewer advertisements. Over here I find the commercials not only repetitious, but also shocking. Before Christmas, I expected feverish claims to be made on the public's every spare penny, but now that the crisis has passed, the avarice of shopkeepers has not abated. There are sales of wilting fir trees, melting snowmen, and jilted turkeys.

Moreover, these are not the worst commercials. It is generally admitted that, during the past twelve years, America has been reduced by its credit-card policies to owing money to almost every other nation on earth, but this way of thinking is still encouraged. Television offers vast loans to people who 'have bad credit or no credit at all'. Similarly, now that it might be possible to persuade even the proselytizing Dr Ruth that sex is a mistake, we are not being encouraged to think about something else, but, instead, are offered inflammatory telephone conversations with women whose smirking faces are constantly shown on our screens. All these blandishments carry warnings that no one under the age of eighteen may avail himself of them, but no suggestion is forthcoming as to how such a restriction can be enforced. If anyone were to make the feeblest attempt to curtail these commercials, there would be an outcry and the citation of any number of Amendments. Perhaps the Amendments should be amended.

Another activity that helps to occupy the time spent waiting for the snow to melt is the writing of letters. Among those that I have most recently received is one from an unknown young man who complains that, while the words 'gay community' are in frequent use, no such happy confederacy exists. His letter lists all the different factions that compose the gay population, but he pours scorn on all of them. Perhaps it may be worthwhile to write down my thoughts in this matter.

I think that anyone who feels reluctantly set apart from his fellow homosexuals must make some effort to accept their idiosyncrasies. He must party with the inveterate partygoers, scream with the screamers, and, if he grows tired of these vigorous activities, he can try visiting the closets of his less extrovert friends.

Most of the week has been spent preparing for my forthcoming visit to Seattle. I have no idea what will be expected of me there, but, on the principle of never saying no to any invitation, I shall go the Alice B. Theater and try to say the words the Washingtonians wish to hear.

Once, just before starting on a plane journey, I remember being involved in a conversation founded entirely on a misunderstanding. Someone asked me if I was in a state of anxiety; I replied that I was. This was taken to mean that I doubted that a heavier-than-air machine could stay up in the sky. In fact, this was not the cause of my furrowed brow. Of course, if a plane I was in suddenly dived towards the earth, I should squeak and cry and pray and show all sorts of signs of panic, but I do not start on a flight worrying about the forces of gravity any more than I wander around the Lower East Side thinking how I will proceed if I am attacked by a stranger. Before a journey by any means of locomotion, I am preoccupied with whether I have packed enough lip gloss to last for the duration of my stay and whether I shall be late because all the bridges leading out of Manhattan are hardly more than picturesque ruins.

In the meantime, I have received a letter from the Ronald

Firbank Society in England. Presumably, it publishes a magazine, because it has asked me to explain in 900 words what has gone wrong with sex. The answer is that sex suffers from the same malaise as television: there is too much of it, with the result that it repeats itself. Halfway through what you had assumed was going to be a new episode, you realize that it's a re-run: you know how it will end. After that, it's difficult to remain interested.

When I was about eight years old, my parents rented, more or less permanently, a cottage in a village called Pett. It was situated about a mile from the Sussex coast. On most days during our annual summer holidays we carried food prepared by my long-suffering mother to the beach where, in considerable discomfort, we ate wasp-infested fruit and sand-encrusted sandwiches. The war was still raging in France, and I distinctly remember that we stood at the water's edge and listened to what Mr Wilfred Owen called 'the monstrous anger of the guns'. Now, looking back, this seems impossible, for they must have been twenty-five miles away, but a mood of mournful curiosity returns to me whenever I recall the horrors of my childhood vacations. Whoever said that children are innocent? Because my sister and my brothers claimed to be eager to bathe, I squeaked with feigned delight whenever I caught sight of the sea, but in fact, I hated it and I still do. The ocean is not my friend. Why does it keep banging away at the helpless shore and making all that noise? What does it want?

To the west of us at Pett beach were the romantic cliffs of Fairlight and the jolly, busy seaside resort of Hastings, but to the east lay Dungeness. The very word is like a knell. If we walked in that direction, we came to Romney Marshes. Gradually the landscape became flatter, the shore grew stonier, the sky darkened, and bird calls assumed a lonely, grieving note. It is in this doom-laden terrain that Mr Derek Jarman has, for some unknown reason, chosen to live, and it is there that his latest movie is set. The landscape serves him well. The film is called *The Garden* – presumably of Gethsemane.

I didn't know that I had ever met Mr Jarman, but he assures me that we were co-judges of a beauty competition held in a London school of art. As I was occasionally a model there, and consequently an object of naked contempt, this seems unlikely, but I dare not doubt him: he is so friendly. Last week, he and his merry men came to my door with one of those vans in which moviemakers habitually travel (and, I suspect, sometimes sleep) and conveyed me to an obscure café at the corner of King and Hudson Streets. There, in a twilit upper room, we drank a few beers and met a few anonymous well-wishers before walking to the Film Forum where *The Garden* was being shown for one night. If this is the only screening in Manhattan of this film, it seems strange that so few of the crowned heads of the industry were present, and so little fuss was made about Mr Jarman, because he is, without doubt, a genius.

I have seen at least one other of his films; it was *The Tempest*, in which David Meyer walked in and out of the North Sea wearing nothing but a sword, and Elisabeth Welch sang 'Stormy Weather'. It was a deliberately skittish rendering of Mr Shakespeare's play, but, for oddity, it had nothing on the new work. *The Garden* is not impish; it is haunting . . . even harrowing.

Its style is what is glibly called surrealistic. Whatever this term suggests to connoisseurs, to real people it means that, by placing them in a deliberately inappropriate setting, an intense reality is bestowed upon objects that most of us take for granted. For instance, a kettle on a stove will be instantly recognized however vaguely it is delineated, but if it is standing in the middle of the Sahara desert, it must proclaim its kettlehood very loudly indeed if it is not to become a pyramid. In *The Garden*, almost all backgrounds are at variance with what is going on in front of them. Everything on which the camera rests its baleful eye acquires an unnatural intensity. On the way home from Hudson Street, I asked the director how this effect was achieved. It seems that it is possible nowadays to photograph people and things against a plain blue backdrop and add a quite different background later. Thus, an absolutely unruffled group of actors can stand beneath a raging, stormy sky or a harshly-lit figure can appear in a misty, nocturnal setting. It is this unreal reality that gives *The Garden* its appealing beauty.

When I returned to Seattle, the people were as friendly as they had been two weeks ago, but the weather was completely different. Having described the city as San Francisco wet, I must now say that it is San Francisco dry – especially when I recall that every morning that I was in the gay Mecca of California, if I looked out of the window when I first awoke, I saw only a dim grey wall of mist. Nothing resembling a landscape emerged until at least high noon. On this visit to Seattle, I was clearly able to see Mr Rainier's mountain; it looked like a negative of Fujiyama – a dark volcanic cone silhouetted against a pale sky.

The journeys there and back were less attractive on this second trip. The airport's spy-catching machine had become as suspicious as a parole officer. Every time I came anywhere near it, it complained loudly until I had given my keys (on which there hangs a huge metal label marked 'SUNDANCE'), my rings, my lipstick, and my money to an appalled attendant. Only then did the machine give me its approval.

Once again, the plane was nowhere near full; this was an advantage, as it permitted a kind stranger named Mr Hubbard to sit beside me and talk. It transpired that he rules an opera star, a Leonie Rysanek, whose photograph will appear on the cover of a forthcoming issue of *Opera Monthly*, so we had quite a large area of common ground to explore. My companion even managed to go a long way towards convincing me to listen kindly to opera.

Wherever I go professionally in the United States, I am always talking to audiences about happiness because it is the only thing that I understand; the only variation is my approach. In Seattle, the management suggested that I should start by explaining myself in general and, in particular, the mystery of my so-belated decision to leave England and settle – if I can call my life here settled – in

America. What seemed to amuse audiences at the Alice B. Theater most was my description of the difference between life in Manhattan and what passes for life in London.

The first thing that every English visitor to New York notices is that here everybody is his friend. Once, when I was travelling innocently up Third Avenue on a bus, a young man crouched beside me and, very discreetly, asked me to write my name on a fragment of paper. I complied with his request and he returned to his seat. Immediately, a large woman sitting on the other side of the bus asked loudly, 'Well, who are you?' Hanging my head in feigned modesty, I replied, 'Who indeed?' This apparently was not a satisfactory answer, because she then said, 'I thought he was asking for your autograph.' Simpering, I admitted that he was.

SHE: Well, why?

ME: You must ask him.

He was sitting with his head in his hands, but no one else within earshot was, so she turned to the entire clientèle of the bus and exclaimed, 'Well, who the hell *is* he?' Nobody actually answered, but they all seemed to be enjoying the dialogue immensely. When the moment came for me to alight, I passed the woman and as I did so, I said, 'I'm sorry I wasn't anybody.' Then even the driver laughed.

Nothing like this would ever occur in Britain. An Englishman once said to me accusingly, 'You're the one who lives in America permanently – why?' I explained that here everybody speaks to everybody everywhere you go. On this remark his comment was, 'I can't think of anything worse.' To demonstrate that this attitude is a national one, I repeat a story told by a friend of mine about a friend of hers.

A woman, intending to make a long journey by rail, went to a main-line terminus in London and, as she was early, entered the station canteen. There she bought a cup of coffee and a Kit Kat. Then she had to negotiate the change, the Kit Kat, the coffee, her shoulder bag, and her suitcase while she looked for somewhere to sit. The only vacant seat that she could see was at a table where someone was already seated, so reluctantly she sat there. After putting down her case and sliding her bag from her shoulder, she put some free sugar and milk into her cup. The Kit Kat was lying in the middle of the table. The moment she unwrapped it and laid it out on its sheet of silver foil, the man opposite her leaned forward, broke off a piece, and ate it. Deeply affronted, she also broke off a piece. Then, while she was taking a few sips from her cup, he took another piece, leaving her only one last bit. This she quickly devoured.

Then the stranger went to the counter and bought himself a cream bun which was a spiral confection with a little disc of pastry on the top. At that moment the woman's train arrived, so she hastily reversed the original ritual, hitched her bag on to her shoulder, took up her suitcase, and, as she passed her enemy, she snatched the lid from his bun and ate it defiantly. Then she boarded the train and, as it moved off, she put her case in the luggage rack, sat down, took her bag on to her lap, opened it, and there was the Kit Kat. The one on the table had, of course, been his, but because he and she were both English and had never been introduced to one another, neither could say, 'What the hell are you doing with my chocolate biscuit?'

The day after my return from the Far West, though as near to collapse as the Brooklyn Bridge, I reconstructed myself for an appointment in a nearby diner with a journalist from a London paper. She wished to question me about my image. Many of my answers were self-evident. There are not many occasions when I can justify my actions with the threadbare excuse, 'Everybody does it,' but this was one of them. For instance, I explained that, like everyone else, I gave up wearing nail varnish when my hands began to look like claws. I was also able to describe myself by quoting other English papers which define me as 'a scruffy dandy', but this, it seemed, was not enough. 'How do you think of yourself ?' my interviewer persisted. I should have replied, 'Incessantly,' but this riposte did not occur to me. For once, words, which I have always regarded as my best friends, failed me.

A totally incongruous mystical element has suddenly entered my life. Last week, a Mr Acosta, a huge gentleman looking like Mr Michelangelo's idea of God but not so worried, arrived on the Lower East Side in a purring limousine, embraced me in the street, and whisked me away to a house of indescribable splendour on East 80th Street.

This extraordinary event resulted from the fact that Mr Acosta and I have apparently met before. On that occasion, he says, he introduced himself to me on Second Avenue, whereupon I replied, 'You must be the unicorn man' – a remark that amazed him because at that time he was involved in a film about one of these mythical beasts. I have no recollection whatsoever of this conversation, but Mr Acosta has never forgotten it, and, thinking of me as in some way in touch with the infinite, while famous names fell like rain from his fur-fringed lips, he showed me extracts from yet another picture that may be categorized as unabashed festival material. It features Mr John Hurt as a bag lady heading a cast consisting entirely of cats, photographed in slow motion and the most lurid lighting ever seen. To Comrade Prokofiev's score, these creatures represent rather than act the story of *Romeo and Juliet*, while some of Mr Shakespeare's lines are recited by real actors. It is Mr Acosta's wish that I should speak a few phrases uttered by a character called Balthasar. Now I will be compelled to read this play, which so far I have only ever scanned in a cursory manner while searching for the answers to crossword clues.

My agent once pointed out to me that if I praise absolutely everything, my judgement will soon be regarded as worthless. She is right, but it is also true that, because I can always be relied upon to say something nice, publishers continue to send me proof copies of their books for a eulogistic 'quote'. It is in this spirit of eternal optimism that Hamish Hamilton has now given me an advance copy of *Rebel Mates*, by Graham McCann.

Some years ago, when I was on a whirlwind tour of provincial cities in England, I met Mr McCann. He looked so young that I secretly thought he was a student. It was as well that I didn't say so, because, in fact, he is a professor. I have no idea what he teaches, but his abiding preoccupation is with the image-making propensities of the cinema. His book about Miss Monroe was the ultimate treatise on the movie star goddess and slave.

His latest work is about Messrs Clift, Brando and Dean. He regards these three actors as having taken over the screen from Mr Wayne and Mr Gable, those icons of total masculinity, and as representing American man's idea of himself since the 1950s — the decade in which the country began to lose its optimism and the Hollywood machine broke down. Mr McCann says that all three of the above-named actors were bisexual, and suggests that this ambiguity was at least in part the cause of that self-doubt that manifested itself in inner conflict and an outward display of unfocused rebellion — that turned Mr Dean into what Mr Kazan called 'a pudding of hatred' and made Mr Brando so perfectly suited to the part of *The Wild One* who, you may remember, when asked, 'What are you rebelling against?', replied, 'What've you got?'

I have never understood the immense popularity of Mr Clift. To me he seemed to be a shrimp with a shrimp's close-set eyes whose idea of acting was to confront the camera with a meaningless stare, but then, I was already middle-aged by the time the Fifties were in full swing; it was much too late in life for me to admire self-doubt.

About once a week, some young person writes to me or telephones me with the suggestion that we should meet. Whenever possible, I comply with his or her request on the principle that we should never say no to anything except an appeal for money, but, just in case the stranger is a murderer, I agree to a rendezvous in a neighbourhood diner. This week I was given lunch by a young man from Brooklyn who was on his way to an audition for a part in yet another of Professor Bentley's plays. We discussed many subjects, and finally talked about the vague but intense feeling that almost all men seem to have of being inhibited by the society in which they live. This is an emotion that I have never felt; I cannot think of anything important that I refrain from doing because of what the world would say.

When I returned home from this very pleasant meeting, I at once began to read Dr McCann's book about Mr Clift *et al*. It then dawned on my befuddled brain that what many men feel convention is preventing them from expressing may not be some hideous piratical urge to rape or homicide, but the feminine side of their natures. This is an idea that has never before occurred to me.

POSTSCRIPT: I have received from Mr Robert Patrick, in Stockton, California, a postcard which states that he has learned how to make a homosexual invisible. 'You may tell your readers,' he writes, 'that if you don't spread disease, exhibit pornographic photographs, or rape and kill small children, they don't know that you exist.'

Whatever will the East Third Street postman think?

Exactly one week after an extraordinary auction at the Cooper Union, in which two seats to hear the nonsense that I talk were sold to the highest bidder, I went to the New York Public Library to fulfil my half of this strange bargain. I didn't do very well, but American audiences are too indulgent to protest.

I was supposed to discourse on the subject of wit, and I have a lot to say on this theme, but I had not properly organized my thoughts. It had been a difficult week. With one hand I had tried to write something kind for *Christopher Street* about a film called *Queens Logic*, which is really a non-movie about a non-place, and, with the other, to explain censorship to the readers of a highly

literary periodical called *The Hungry Mind*, which is published in
St Paul, Minnesota. In my by no means humble opinion, restric-
tions are essential not only in society (a notion that most people
seem to accept), but also in the arts (which young people find
irksome, if not intolerable). It is my contention that artists, in
whatever medium, produce flabbier work the more freedom they
are given: all subtlety, all irony vanishes. For instance, Miss West
ascended the throne in a decade when moralists grew on palm
trees in Hollywood. She was compelled to use considerable skill
to imply what she was forbidden to say. Proof of her greatness
lies in the fact that the line, 'Come up and see me sometime,' has
passed for ever into the folklore of filth because of her delivery of
the phrase – which, in itself, contains not one word that a nun
would be reluctant to utter. Preoccupation with these weighty
matters took up much of the time and energy that ought to have
been devoted to organizing what I wanted to say about humorous
writing.

I had no idea that my arrival at the library would receive so
much attention. On 42nd Street, an unknown woman was lurking
in the shadow of the stone lions, waiting to ask me to write a
foreword to a book about a drag artist of whom nobody has ever
heard. I suggested that she should telephone me so that, in calmer
circumstances, I could explain to her that I would gladly do almost
anything (for a fee) if and when it was quite certain that this
improbable biography would one day be published. At the very
door of the building, another unknown woman begged me to take
her in with me, although the place was rumoured to be full.

The gentleman who had organized this assignment had miracu-
lously found for me a copy of *Vile Bodies* by Mr Waugh. It is the
funniest book ever written, and I had hoped to quote long passages
from it to fill the silences left by my ineptitude. I had read this
book sixty years ago, when it was first published and when I still
read books wantonly. I did not then realize that it was satire; I
loved all those feckless bright young things. When I looked at it
again, I saw that it was far too full of mordant English irony to

appeal to Americans. For instance, it says of a fictitious fashionable eating place, 'Chez Espinosa . . . was full of oilcloth and Lalique glass, and the sort of people who liked that sort of thing went there continually and said how awful it was.' This single sentence encapsulates the attitude adopted by what the press used to call 'café society'. Over there, disdain is considered chic. Over here, the opposite is true; the national characteristic of the United States is indiscriminate enthusiasm. I didn't manage to put any of these opinions in an orderly manner; I merely flung myself into the well-known smiling and nodding racket.

The best part of the evening began when the performance was over. Then the organizers of the evening took the winners of the auction lot and me to a small but delightful restaurant called Tout Va Bien; it is on 51st Street between Eighth and Ninth Avenues. There we ate and drank and talked for hours without the management appearing to grow restless. Towards the end of the evening, one of the guests, suddenly deciding that the occasion must be immortalized, went to the telephone and summoned a photographer. Within fifteen minutes, two girls and a camera arrived to take our pictures. What worldly power!

I have failed. I never had much to recommend me except that I keep my word, so I am very conscientious about paying my bills as soon as they arrive, acknowledging gifts that come by mail, and keeping appointments. But last week I defaulted. Some time ago, I had received a kind invitation from the Baroness Sherry von Korber-Bernstein to a birthday celebration at Club 53. She is one of the people on the peanut circuit that I most admire and I was looking forward eagerly to the occasion. The day before the event, she even telephoned me to make sure that I would be there and I promised that I would, but, on the appointed evening, it snowed. I had even reconstructed myself and gone downstairs to the front door, but when I saw the weather in the street, I lost my nerve. I returned to my room, dismantled myself, had a good cry, and went to bed.

I am frightened of the snow. Like many people of my age, I dread slippery or uneven surfaces; if I were to fall and break even the smallest bone, it would never mend; I am no longer renewable. I would write to her a humble letter if I knew the Baroness's address, but, as with so many Americans, that seems to be a secret. I cannot, therefore, ease my conscience by making my apologies.

The following day the snow ceased to fall, so at the request of a Mr Jones I did go to the Limelight to meet all the virgins of New York. I didn't see any girls in flowing white robes carrying lilies. In fact, though the décor of the place looked different, the clientèle seemed exactly the same as last time I was there. However, I was rewarded by sitting next to a lady who told me that the love of her life was her cat and that, when one of her gentlemen friends suggested that she should transfer her affection to him, she replied that, if he was willing to undergo the operation that had been performed on her pet, she would consider his proposition.

I returned home from the virgins to find that the war in the Persian Gulf was over – at least in the opinion of various televisionaries. I personally regard all this rejoicing as somewhat premature; I think this period of American history will one day come to be called 'The Elba Fallacy'. (Elba, it should be recalled, was the island from which Mr Bonaparte returned to make more trouble.)

1991

Spring

*

*Though sex seems still to be with us, breasts have
once again subsided*

Time passes more swiftly in America than elsewhere. If a public
building is fifteen years old, plans are made to demolish it; if an
actress hasn't made a movie in a whole year, she must make a
'comeback'; in England, her return to the screen would only be
described in those terms if she had been absent from it for six
years. This national awareness of the speed with which time is
passing may be due to Americans having short memories, and
that, in turn, is why they hunger for a recorded past.

To satisfy this need, Manhattan has become an island on which
every fifth person is a photographer who takes at least thirty
pictures of every subject, however trivial. This state of affairs is a
source of amazement to me. Photography is such a complicated
profession; it requires a knowledge of chemistry and of physics.
Furthermore, it necessitates the buying of equipment so expensive
that it has to be insured, and the renting of premises that yield a
large uninterrupted space with big windows, and when all these
circumstances have been assembled, the end product is only an
imitation of life.

Last week, the day of reckoning came for which I had been prepared
by a sumptuous tea at the Helmsley Palace given to me by my
mad moviemaker, Mr Acosta (mentioned in an earlier entry in
this journal). He took me to lunch at Joe Allen's restaurant on
West 46th Street to fortify me for a visit to a recording studio,
which turned out to be but a stone's throw away – and it was a

wonder that stones were not thrown. There I spoke various lines from Mr Shakespeare's *Romeo and Juliet*. Not all of these are uttered in the play by the same character, but Mr Acosta is dauntless. He is also inexhaustibly patient.

We arrived in the torture chamber at two o'clock in the afternoon, and did not leave until after half past four. The endless re-takes were, of course, entirely my fault, but no one evinced the slightest irritation with me. My own reaction to this situation has been, from the very beginning, one of complete bewilderment. As everybody knows, my voice is as flat as a pancake, though not as palatable. Why ever was I being asked to recite poetry that has taxed the skills of great actors? I bleated the lines over and over again on one side of a sound-proof glass wall while, on the other, Mr Acosta, as though conducting an orchestra, tried to coax from my flaccid vocal cords some hint of music, some breath of magic. If he had not been due somewhere else at five o'clock, we would still be in that studio. If my performance is ultimately used, which doesn't seem very likely, it will be woven with the voices of Miss Smith, Miss Redgrave, Mr Kingsley, and other luminaries of the movie industry. How angry they will be!

When this session was over, a large white cat was released from a container, and I was photographed with it. As this movie will be acted entirely by Mr Hurt and a bunch of cats, presumably this creature was the juvenile lead. Whether this picture was a serious publicity shot or a joke, I did not dare to ask.

As long as I can wrest from the hands of fate at least one day a week during which I do not leave my room, and therefore am not obliged to devote several hours to reconstructing myself for public viewing, it doesn't really matter which day of the week it is. I do not go regularly to an office, and seldom do any serious shopping, so I don't even mind if my self-imposed imprisonment occurs on a Saturday, but if it does, there is one disadvantage. Television regards weekends as mini-Christmases. Except for the news, which never fails to regale us with stories of domestic folly and global disaster, programmes during that time tend to be very bland. Last Saturday, I spent the daylight hours trying to explain that interior decoration is folly to one magazine and, to another, that music is a sin. Then, when night fell, I watched television with half an eye. I was just about to abandon all hope of entertainment when a cops-and-robbers movie, called *Arizona Heat*, began.

At first this appeared to be a cosy but hardly original tale about a policeman who is known for his unconventional – even scandalous – methods of bringing justice to the city, but who cannot be dismissed from the force because of his high average of successful arrests. My interest was enhanced when he was given a female partner on the grounds that her presence would civilize the wild beast in him. Even then I thought this would only provide a mixture of violence and sex, but no.

One fine morning, our hero calls at his partner's home and is introduced to her flat-mate, an airline stewardess. This situation arouses his suspicions (and mine); pretending he needs to go to the bathroom, he peeps slyly into the bedroom and sees the incriminating double bed. Suddenly, the movie adds to its customary cinematographic realism an entirely different kind of human reality. Once the partner has admitted that she is a lesbian, the rogue cop cannot leave the subject alone.

Both his and her characters are exceedingly well drawn, and their dialogue is entirely free from political or poetic generalities. *Arizona Heat* survived its fatuous title and became, at least in my experience, the first movie ever to show us – nay, to force upon us – a painful glimpse of what it is like to be an unavailable woman in an obsessively masculine world. Life is much harder for self-confessed homosexual women than for gay men. If I had not enjoyed a fairly lazy day, I would never have stayed up late enough to see that film. The moral is: Never go to bed early on a Saturday night.

The letter of the week comes from a boy aged thirteen living in an unknown town in the middle of Germany. He had read some gossip about me in a recent issue of a magazine called *Stern*. He says that convinced him that I am 'a funny man' (to say the least) and he demands a long reply from me telling him what I like and don't like.

What makes this communication so remarkable is firstly that anyone so young could be bothered to write to such a freakish character as I and could be so cosmopolitan as to be interested in anyone in such a distant land. Secondly, there is not one spelling error and there are only a few erroneously used parts of speech. Almost no letter that I receive from people twice his age in any state of America is, in this academic sense, so correct. Is there something wrong with American education?

Some kind friends whom I once visited in Indiana send me newspapers that they receive regularly from England so that I may fritter away my time attempting to solve the elaborate crossword puzzles that they contain. Occasionally, I break my vow of ignorance and allow my gaze to fall on the news. In this way, I recently stumbled upon one of the funniest items of useless information that I have ever read. A rich English eccentric (famous for having taken Salvador Dali seriously) was said to have hated his mother. He can hardly be blamed for this if the following anecdote is an example of the depth of her interest in her offspring. One Sunday morning, while dressing with great care before going to church, she demanded that one of her children accompany her. When asked (presumably by a governess), 'Which child?', she replied, 'Whichever one goes with my blue dress.'

It is precisely such outlandish tales as this that give Americans the impression that the British indulge their eccentrics. They do, but with one important qualification. These human national treasures must be rich, or, if not well-heeled, at least well-born. Even in this outfield of English society, snobbery still reigns supreme. Oddity among one's social equals is regarded as 'putting on airs'. It gives rise to such questions as, 'Who the hell do you think you are that you may disregard the rules which, however irksome, the rest of us have agreed to obey?' Another remark frequently made in these circumstances is, 'What would happen to the world if everyone behaved as you do?' – a foolish query when what has provoked all this indignation is an instance of unique behaviour.

The name of Julie Harris is for ever engraved upon my heart because of a small incident that took place during my first visit to Los Angeles. In some vast building the name and exact location of which I have long since forgotten, the crowned heads of Hollywood had gathered to bear witness to the presentation of yet another award to Miss Harris. I was there with Mr Hillard Elkins, and I asked him whether she had already arrived and, if so, whether I might touch the hem of her garment. He crossed the entire room to where she was sitting and asked if she would permit this. She rose immediately and came to our table. I cannot think of any other celebrity who would have bothered to do this. Miss Harris is the personification of 'noblesse oblige'.

When we met last week, she had completely forgotten this occasion for the simple reason that it was just an expression of the way she is all the time. I know this now because on Monday I was taken by her goddaughter to see Miss Harris's latest one-person show, Lucifer's Child, and afterwards we accompanied her and other guests to the Russian Tea Room, that haunt of celebrities next to Carnegie Hall, where the goddaughter spends most of her spare time, as though it were her local diner. The show, at the Music Box Theater, tells the life story of the Baroness Karen von Blixen-Finecke, who, under the pen name Isak Dinesen, wrote Out of Africa and whom Miss Streep played in the movie of that name. The present show takes place much later in the Baroness's life – long after Robert Redford is dead and she has returned to her ancestral home in Denmark. The woman we see now is less romantic, more cynical, and much deeper in the clutches of the disease she contracted from her husband.

Lucifer's Child is very ingeniously devised by a Mr Luce. During the first act, the Baroness packs for her visit to America, and this provides Miss Harris with a lot to do and the audience with things to see as well as hear. Like all one-person shows, this is fundamentally an exercise in lovability, and of this art, Miss Harris, though neither coy nor sentimental, is a master.

Supper at the Russian Tea Room after the show was, in a sense, an even more engaging experience. Miss Harris is totally without affectation – a trait that I find remarkable in a famous actress – and she is an amalgam of contradictory qualities: strong but almost alarmingly frail, self-possessed but able to take an interest in everything said to her. For me, the entire evening was, in its quiet way, a truly memorable occasion.

Sooner or later the time comes for almost everybody when, although he has sworn to himself that he will never utter such sentiments, he declares that the country is going to the dogs, that life has become louder, public manners cruder, and art totally incomprehensible. Where, he asks himself, will it all end? I began to lose my grip on culture with the poems of Mr Eliot, the plays of Mr Beckett, and the novels of Mr Joyce. Then one day last week, in spite of all my efforts to prevent such a disaster, I finally fell into the abyss of bewilderment.

Mr Jack Eric Williams accompanied me to the La MaMa Theater to see a play, or at least an event, entitled *Eddy Goes to Poetry City*, by a Mr Foreman. As far as I could tell, no one was given a programme and no one bought a ticket – a bad sign, but a ruse that disarms criticism. The performance space was decorated with great care to look as hideous as possible, and in it a cast of five people, obviously rehearsed with the utmost care, moved about, sometimes quite violently, and, wearing strange devices that amplified their voices alarmingly, declaimed various aphoristic phrases. At the end, a surprisingly large audience applauded enthusiastically.

As we left, someone who had driven all the way from the very edge of Long Island for this experience asked Mr Williams what the play had meant. (I'd say he had the right to know.) I did not hear the reply because I tottered home abruptly in a state of collapse, but I asked the same question by telephone the next day. I have now been informed that Mr Foreman calls his company The Ontological/Hysteric Theater, and he is concerned with the interpenetrability of everything, atomized; Mr Williams called it 'the mind/body split'.

It's such a relief to know.

When children get together, they talk about how awful their teachers are; when wives get together, they talk about how awful their husbands are; and when writers congregate, the common topic of conversation is the failings of their agents. I must have been lucky; I've had two agents and never felt the least animosity towards either of them. My first agent I never truly understood, but then he was a Hungarian and I'm grateful to him for putting me into the smiling and nodding racket. Without ever knowing it, he prepared me for my American life. My present agent is a saint and also a friend. We meet from time to time whether there is any business to discuss or not. She feeds me and occasionally takes me to parties. Last week we went to the West Side Arts Theater – an establishment not quite up to the gilt-cupids-and-crimson-plush standard, but above the dim cellar level. We were there to see a Mr Reynolds in *Only The Truth Is Funny*.

This is yet another one-man show. When I was young, in this particular field of entertainment there was only Miss Ruth Draper. She was famous to incorrigible theatre-goers, but I do not think she ever attempted the six-evenings-and-two-matinées routine; I believe she most often did afternoons on stages that, at night, were occupied by real plays.

As far as I know, it was the Edinburgh Festival that started the present rage for one-man shows; it became a hothouse for egomaniacs too uncontrollable to work with other actors. Their acts may take any one of several different forms. Miss Draper filled the empty space around her with imaginary characters; most modern solo performers imitate some famous person – Emily

Dickinson, Mr Twain, at a pinch St Matthew, or, more recently, Baroness von Blixen and Mr Capote.

Until someone invented Lily Tomlin and Jackie Mason, I do not think any stand-up comic ever tried to stay the pace for an entire evening – except, possibly, at home. Now Mr Mason has a rival. Mr Reynolds cleverly combines the typical digressions of a stand-up comic with telling us the story of his life. At one point during his performance, he divides the world into assholes and creeps. (He is not squeamish about the words he uses or the events he describes.) Assholes, he tells us, are people who enjoy jokes about physical deformity; creeps are those who do not. I must now admit, with head bowed in shame, that I am the creepiest of them all: I don't even like to hear fun made of victims who are plain or uneducated or of low degree. (In England, I hated *Punch* because in every issue it contained at least one joke about a domestic servant misusing or mispronouncing a word.)

Mr Reynolds is a self-confessed – nay, a self-proclaimed – asshole. His monologue is less depraved than even a few minutes of Lenny Bruce, but it is deliberately, uproariously coarse. In spite of this, his overall message is that life is worth living and that love is wonderful. The audience, though neither exclusively male nor predominantly young, believed him wholeheartedly. Personally, though I admired Mr Reynold's energy and his untiring voice, I was embarrassed.

On the day following my visit to the Actors Playhouse, I was invited by Mr Tony Origlio, who once undertook the hazardous task of publicizing me, to eat at The Ballroom on West 28th Street, and, after lunch, to watch a cabaret act performed by Mr Julian Clary. The food and the show were equally appetizing.

Mr Clary comes to us from a triumphant six-week stint at the Aldwych Theatre in London. He is an example of what might be termed the 'New Wave' of gay entertainers. This is not a drag show. Mr Clary makes no attempt to impersonate famous female actresses or, indeed, anybody at all; he remains invincibly himself and unmistakably English. He is as much made up as the forces of gravity will permit, and he wears clothes of no particular sex so glittering that, from time to time, rays of light from his body hit you in the eye like gleams that fall from those mirrored globes that revolve about certain dance floors. In an unashamed suburban English accent, a barrage of innuendoes falls from his ruby lips; he renders rather than sings a few numbers with titles such as 'I Want To Be A Rhinestone Cowboy' and occasionally, though he cannot be described as dancing, he raises an arm or a leg like a little boy performing in a drawing room for his mother's guests. The effect is absurd, endearing, and absolutely unique.

While I was sitting innocently in my favourite diner on East Fifth Street being photographed, an unknown gentleman approached me and accused me of doing a disservice to the movie called *Paris Is Burning* when I wrote about it for a recent edition of the *New York Times*. Since that terrible day, I have learned that almost the entire population of Manhattan (including Mr Musto, whose opinions I hold sacred) is up in arms concerning my view of this picture. I am worried by this public reaction because no such negative effect was intended. After seeing this documentary at The Film Forum, I met its director, Miss Livingston, and liked her immediately – besides which, I praise everything on principle.

I have now rolled about under the bed in my room, retrieved the carbon copy of my review, and re-read it. It says that *Paris Is Burning* is 'hilarious on the surface and, underneath the glitter, profoundly sad; it speaks with the fierce bravado that is the voice of society's permanent exiles.' These words are a somewhat high-flown paraphrase of the explanation given to me by Miss Livingston of the events in her film. Later, my review describes the picture as 'funny, frightening, and tragic'. In all that I wrote, there is not one word of opprobrium. What did I do wrong?

Naturally, I endeavoured to see this movie through the eyes of a typical Sunday *Times* reader, because that was the paper to which I was contributing. I do not pretend that journalism is an art, but I do think it is a skill to give readers what they wish to hear while claiming to present stark, unbiased truth. To justify his rage, the unknown gentleman in the diner cried out, 'The people in the film are doing what you did.' This is true, and, like them, I also was regarded by readers of the *Times* as funny, frightening, and tragic – if not downright disgusting.

Last week, I was taken by a teacher of architecture to Yale University. It was a most enjoyable outing – a drive through the New England countryside, lunch at the most oddly-designed school canteen in the world, and an unexpected opportunity to meet Mr Edmund White, whose contributions to various kinky magazines I had been reading for some years past, but whom I had never before seen with the naked eye.

We were assembled with two or three other people to comment on the ways in which about eight students of the architectural faculty had met the challenge of designing a school for 'gay' teenagers. The answers, of course, took the form of drawings, plans, elevations, and models of hypothetical buildings. Mr White had pertinent remarks to make about them. I, alas, had no idea whether these proposals were examples of good or bad architecture; to me a building is only a box in which to store one's body when not in use. Presumably, I was present in the hope that I would say something witty.

I failed. At first, my reaction was merely amazement at the skill with which the models had been constructed; it aroused in me the same wonder that I feel when I see galleons in bottles. Later, I grew surprised that the project had been set in the first place. My father never took the slightest interest in me or my education, but if he ever had moved his thin lips to ask me of what my studies consisted and I had replied that I was building a school for a bunch of homosexual children, he would at once have demanded the return of my school fees. At Yale, there was apparently neither panic nor perplexity.

Finally, on the way back to New York, I began to feel sad that, when each student tried to explain his work, he was almost unintelligible. Each must have known in advance that some verbal justification of his efforts would be expected of him, but all seemed quite unprepared. If I had taken anything seriously on that day, this would have depressed me deeply. I had not hoped for deathless oratory, but I had also not expected a flow of 'ums', 'ers', and false starts from the lips of the most privileged young men in the world.

An unknown gentleman has written to me concerning my views on American education, saying that all teaching is firstly the teaching of language. I agree with him. Muddled syntax is the outward and audible sign of confused minds, and the misuse of grammar the result of illogical thinking.

I have been approached by the editor of a magazine that I had thought extinct, but it is not and I have been asked to write an article explaining four movie actresses from the past: Jayne Mansfield, Marilyn Monroe, Diana Dors and Kim Novak.

Reading the condensed biographies of these ladies, all of whom were born either in the late Twenties or early Thirties, I realized that until the Fifties when all of them emerged into the klieg lights, apart from Miss West, who defied all the rules, no American actress had serious breasts. In the movie *Queen Christina*, Miss Garbo had to stand under a specially focused light before Mr John Gilbert could tell that she was a woman. (Miss Mansfield would never have attempted the masquerade in the first place.) Even Miss Dietrich, who represented femininity at an intensity never previously known, had legs but no breasts.

The obscene interest evinced by Hollywood publicists in what they evasively termed the 'vital statistics' of movie stars was, of course, yet another symptom of the sexual explosion that dealt the death blow of romance about thirty-five years ago. Of these four actresses, only the name of Miss Monroe now still rouses the public imagination. Miss Mansfield and Miss Dors were famous in their day, but only for the generous way in which they connived with the public at the joke about the bust measurements. For this reason, they were among the few female stars better known and better liked by men than women.

Now, though sex seems still to be with us, breasts have once again subsided. This is hard to explain. I dare not hope that we are at last returning to a less carnal era. In Miss Mansfield's day, breasts were never seen naked by the cine-camera. It may, therefore, have seemed necessary to imply by sheer bulk what could not actually be shown. Now that nudity is everywhere and almost all movies contain prolonged sequences of sexual antics, however gratuitously introduced, the mere size of any particular erogenous zone may no longer matter. (The vital statistics of male stars are not yet published, but dry your tears: the day will come.)

Miss Novak is even harder to explain than the vanishing breasts. She had neither a bosom nor legs, but at one time her appeal was greater than that of Doris Day, Grace Kelly, or even the invincible Miss Taylor. At first, unlike Miss Mansfield, she was in successful films such as *The Man with the Golden Arm*. The script for this picture was so ludicrous that, at the end of it, two cops with soppy expressions on their faces watch the lovers, both of whom are wanted for questioning in a murder case, sauntering off into the distance. But the story was about drug addiction, which at that time was all the rage. Miss Novak's later movies were less success-ful, but if she had been a true star, when the surrounding night darkened, her image would have glowed more brightly than ever. Unfortunately, this did not happen.

Last Friday I was sitting innocently in my room typing a review of *Miss Saigon* when I was interrupted by a telephone call from a Mr Marder who traffics in improbable movies. Only half-listening, I heard that my tickets to yet another film festival would be delivered to me immediately. An hour later, when I went down-stairs to retrieve the mysterious envelope from the floor of our lobby, I found that it contained not, as I had foolishly assumed, cinema tickets, but airline tickets – and to Seattle!

This immediately threw me into a panic. I flung aside my quill pen and began what Mr Debussy would have entitled 'L'Après-Midi d'un Phone'. I succeeded (I hope) in excusing myself gracefully from all the appointments that had been set up for Saturday, Sunday and Monday, except one, which concerned a Mr Max whose telephone number has been changed or declared null and void. As I have never been sure of his surname, I could not search for it in the Manhattan directory, and so have been compelled by forces beyond my feeble control to break my appointment with him.

I am heartbroken. If it had not been for this load of guilt that I carried with me, my sojourn in Seattle would have been most enjoyable. At this time of the year, this fair city hosts a film festival that lasts four whole weeks. Within minutes of arriving in the state of Washington, I was being interviewed by various local papers before going into the Egyptian Theater to see *Lonely In America*. This movie is about a young Indian who comes from Calcutta to live with his uncle in Jackson Heights. It is directed by that Mr Brown who edited *Do the Right Thing* and *Truth or Dare*, and it describes amusingly and wistfully the problem that seems to beset all young people arriving from India: they want to become American as fast as possible, but always find themselves living with and working for their elders who wish to remain Indian for as long as possible and even want the younger generation to enter into marriages arranged at their birth.

The real purpose of my visit to the Far West was so that I could be held responsible for the newest and first full-length 'documentary' film about me. This is called *Resident Alien*. I warned the audience that this picture shows no burning police cars and no hospital nurses being raped in car parks – nothing, in fact, that could be termed family entertainment, but I said that it would offer interesting glimpses of Mr Sting, Mr Hurt (who is my representative on earth), Miss Penny Arcade, Mr Robert Patrick, and sundry other colourful denizens of the Lower East Side of Manhattan. Between movies in Seattle, I met a Mr Whitten, who, against all odds, has secured a booking for *Resident Alien* in

August at the Village Cinema. I cannot imagine how it will fare at the hands of real critics.

Now from England comes a paperback copy of *How To Grow Old Disgracefully*, the autobiography of Miss Hermione Gingold. As she admits – nay, boasts – that at the age of eighty-one she had a twenty-six-year-old lover, this seems an apt title. I read her story with great amusement and was specially pleased to note that her opinion of the difference between British and Americans corresponds closely to mine. She says that if you wear a mink coat in the States, everyone (who isn't an animal freak) admires it, but in England, they say, 'We'll have that off your back, come the revolution.'

On Sunday, some kind friends took me to the very edge of Manhattan where we boarded *The Spirit of New York* for a mini-cruise, which included brunch and a cabaret provided by the catering staff. The weather, though shaky, refrained from behaving badly and I think we all had a pleasant afternoon. For me, the high point of the occasion came when a large gentleman came to our table to tell my host that it was rumoured that there was a celebrity on board who was 'coming out'. Turning to me, he added, 'It can't be you.'

Summer

*

Never, NEVER go to Boston

On the last Saturday in June I went with a friend to a church on Central Park West at 75th Street. We were there to join in what a programme described as a Celebration of Commitment between my friend's sister and her friend, a Miss Haney. I am not a Christian; indeed, I believe only in what I can see – and not all of that. When, long ago, I asked my niece why she was getting married, she replied that, if she didn't, she would be given no presents. So perhaps my general cynicism is a family tradition. All the same, I must admit that when I entered the Church on Central Park West I was nervous.

As soon as I stood in the chancel and saw, over the altar, a vast picture of Jesus of Nazareth washing the feet of his disciples, I remembered that I had been on this hallowed ground before. I had even taken part in a dialogue with one of the church's officials in the presence of a small congregation. I do not recall what was said on that day; I only remember adopting a minimum risk policy. On this more recent occasion, the same stratagem seemed to have been employed. Marriage was not mentioned; the commitment of the two young women to each other was described as a spiritual covenant, but echoes of the wedding service could be heard. I do not think that any but the most thin-lipped Christians could have been offended. It was a joyous but entirely decorous occasion.

Independence Day celebrates the onset of a war that, being still a part-time Englishman, I cannot claim to have won. Therefore, on previous Fourths of July I have cowered in my room, but last

Thursday, at ten o'clock in the morning, I was summoned to some recording studios on Fifth Avenue occupied by the British Broadcasting Corporation. There I took part in a programme the purpose of which was to explain to the English what makes America the way it is.

I felt totally outclassed, because I was co-starred with a Mr London, who teaches American history at New York University, and a Mr Bischoff, who is one of the editors of the *Village Voice*. I said that the uniqueness of the Americans lies in their belief that personality is the greatest power on earth and, in response to other similar questions, uttered all the well-worn aphorisms that I habitually trot out when under fire. I doubt that the British public was much impressed by anything I said, but our interviewer was kind enough to telephone me the next day to tell me that the response from Broadcasting House in London to our efforts had been favourable and that all the participants will be paid. I can't ask for more than that.

In the evening of the same day, as I was returning home from dinner with a friend, we found our block positively glittering with fireworks and, although television has repeatedly warned us all that the buying, selling or igniting of these strident emblems of merriment is illegal, we saw half a dozen policemen standing on the corner of the street and smiling benignly at the flagrant display of lawlessness.

Sad to say, last weekend I had to decline a kind invitation from Jack Eric Williams, who offered to persuade one of his unsuspecting friends to transport us by car into the countryside. I do not hold with nature, but I would gladly have overcome my revulsion from leaves and blades of grass in the hope of escaping for a while from the oven-like atmosphere of the city. This was not to be. Instead, I was compelled to choose between sitting in my room naked with the door shut, thus forfeiting even the hope of a breeze wafting past me, or leaving the door open and wearing clothes so as not to disgust any fellow inmates of the house who might chance to pass by. I tried both these courses of inaction and, in each case, spent most of Saturday and Sunday flopping about with my hair clinging to my forehead, a pool of sweat accumulating in my navel and testicles hanging down to my knees while I attempted to become acquainted with the contents of eight full pages of typescript so that, on the following day, I might be able to orate them with feigned spontaneity before a television camera. I presume my listless performance is to be part of a culture programme to be released in Britain very late at night.

The next morning, I spent the early hours blotting out the pools of perspiration on my face with powder with much the same distaste and with about the same amount of sporadic success as that with which the police cover with sand the grim signs of a street accident. By ten o'clock, a car had arrived to transport me to an address on Sixth Avenue. This turned out to be the home of a photographer and a sculptress. It covered the entire top floor of the building and was a whole world of loosely defined areas linking eating and working spaces. From the middle of it all springs up a spiral staircase leading to a flat roof so densely afforested that it was a wonder that all that exotic vegetation did not cause the edifice to topple over into the street.

With unflagging good nature, our hosts allowed not only me but also a cast of thousands of cameramen, sound-recordists, and general organizers to swarm all over their home for most of the day. When all had been said and all had been recorded, we went to Brooklyn so that I could be photographed trying to look noble against a distant backdrop of the Statue of Liberty and various ferry boats meandering hither and thither. Let no one ever speak ill of New York taxi drivers. In spite of all sorts of hazards, two of them, like charioteers in Mr Hur's movie, consented to drive abreast from the middle of Sixth Avenue to the very edge of Brooklyn merely so that I could be photographed seeming to enjoy the scenery as we sped through the city and over the picturesque ruin that used to be the Brooklyn Bridge. The entire undertaking was not completed until evening, and a benediction of rain had begun to fall upon us. Then, at last, I was released at my front door.

I slept until dawn.

At this time of year, letters fly into Manhattan from California as abundantly and with as much regularity as geese migrating from the frozen north to warmer regions of the world. These missives are all a-flutter and a-twitter with news about the various gay activities that have taken place on the streets of San Francisco. I have a spy living on Sacramento Street who informs me that, this year, the crowds attending all those parades and public events were more numerous than ever before (more than half a million by some estimates) and that the general atmosphere was happier than in recent times. He does not express any misgivings about this phenomenon, but I find it difficult to suppress a feeling of foreboding. If the rest of the population in that state ever conceives of itself as a beleaguered minority, will it not move from its present attitude of armed neutrality to a terrified and terrifying hostility?

I was in Boston last Sunday to lend my gracious presence to another showing of *Resident Alien*. It is hard to believe that my presence really makes the slightest difference to the success of this picture, but as I try never to say no to anything, I did my stint. The film was screened twice, and it is true that the first house at seven-thirty was full, but I think I ought to add that the cinema holds only a hundred and forty people.

I set out from Manhattan on this fateful mission at half past one in the afternoon to catch Mr Trump's three o'clock shuttle from La Guardia airport. (I was amused to learn that the crossword puzzle in his airline magazine consists almost entirely of the names of famous industrialists criss-crossing those of successful business tycoons and manufacturing moguls.) I was met in Boston by a Mr Mansour and his assistant. Mr Mansour rules the Boston Festival with one hand, and with the other, several New York cinemas such as Cinema Twelve and The Village Cinema.

The journey by air was so short that there was no time for the service of a meal, so we ate something before arriving at The Institute, where I was interviewed by the *Boston Phoenix*, *Gay Community News* (whose representative wore white gloves), and by the *Boston Herald*. All this occupied every minute until the first showing of *Resident Alien*, preceded by *A Letter to Harvey Milk*, a documentary made from a short story by a Miss Newman, who was present to introduce it. The two films constituted a double-feature lasting two hours, and Mr Mansour very thoughtfully made it possible for me to avoid seeing my film for a third time (I already knew who won). While it was being screened, he, his assistant, a heap – or should I say pride? – of journalists, and I crept away to eat at a very pleasant restaurant called Ciao Bella. We returned to our duties just in time to answer questions from the audience concerning what they had seen and to introduce the second house.

On reaching my hotel, I flopped into bed exhausted but happy, having spent the past six hours either talking or eating – my two favourite pastimes. The next morning, I arose and reconstructed myself just in time for one final interview, this time with the *Boston Globe*. The city is certainly going to know I was there.

Then the trouble began. Arriving at the airport, I found that Mr Trump had decided to take the latest hurricane warnings seriously. (Why, when he has so successfully ignored such a large number of other prophecies of doom?) When I presented my return ticket, a young woman told me that there would be no flights to New York until two o'clock. 'If then,' she added with barely concealed relish. On hearing this terrifying news, I made a great mistake. I found two other unsuspecting victims and went with them to Boston's South Station, the railway station. There I was forbidden to try to board the first available train on the grounds that it was full. Never before having heard such a flimsy excuse for being obstructive, I said that I would gladly – nay, eagerly – stand all the way back to real life. The ticket-seller did not even bother to reply; he offered me a seat on the 1.35 train or nothing.

Notoriety has its rewards. Having two and a half hours to wait, I began to wander disconsolately about the public area of the station. Half-hearted efforts have been made by the municipal authorities to give this bleak space a jaunty air. A few brightly coloured kites hang from the dingy glass roof, and here and there are small circular tables with large umbrellas sprouting from their centres. From what these are intended to shelter us I cannot imagine. While surveying this incongruous scene, I met a stranger who not only offered me a cup of coffee and a bun, but was good enough to chat with me for an hour. No sooner had he escaped than I was recognized by a self-confessed interior decorator who had seen me at the Town House in Manhattan. He looked after me and fed me during the entire remainder of our ordeal.

At about two o'clock, we were permitted to board the next train bound for New York, but even this massive, earth-bound vehicle was afraid of the hurricane and refused to take the shorter coastal route. It is true that the wind and rain were tempestuous. In fact, the only thing lacking from the scene was a glimpse of Miss Lamour, in a wringing wet sarong, clinging to a bent palm tree. All the same, I would not have expected these climatic manifestations to prompt a train driver to meander inland. There, fallen trees lay across the tracks like palm fronds placed before the feet of returning conquerors with the result that we sat in that train for nine hours.

The moral of this woeful tale is obvious: Never, *never* go to Boston.

The only actual event in my life at the moment is that I am to be made immortal in bronze, or, to be more realistic, ephemeral in clay. This is the second time I have been honoured in this manner since I came to the United States. The first sculptor to approach me saw me working at SNAFU, a dim nightclub which stood where Lox Around the Clock now flourishes. He was an extremely attractive gentleman who unfortunately decided to pare away much of his alluring roly-polyness by joining Overeaters Anonymous. I tried to teach him that people are lovable by the pound, but he paid no heed. He has now taken up residence in Los Angeles, which is, of course, 'thin city'.

The more recent sculptor who has decided to make of me a graven image is a young woman who lives on the Upper East Side, where she hires space in a large communal studio divided into small work areas – an arrangement of which I have never before heard. She very kindly spares me the arduous chore of sitting still for hours. Like most modern portraitists, she works mainly from photographs and adds a few hills and valleys to my face from life when the bulk of the work is done. In a time gone by, art and photography were enemies. Painters and sculptors despised mere snapshots, but during the past few decades, since machines have more or less made human beings redundant, the camera has been redeemed and is now as sacred as canvas or marble.

It isn't quite accurate to describe either of these two artists as sculptors; they are both modellers, members of quite a different profession. The work of a carver is eternal – more or less. He is usually a big man with huge hands and tends to be a patient hermit prepared to remain alone in his studio, wrestling with one project for years on end – one of an altogether more serious breed of men.

My bookish life continues. Mr de Luca, who rules the publicity department of St Martin's Press, has sent me two of its latest books. One, still in the form of an uncorrected proof, is called *Profiles in Gay and Lesbian Courage*, and the other, *Mother Earth*. The first is by the Reverend Troy Perry and a Mr Swicegood. Both these men seem to be wild characters – especially the preacher; he has been married, fathered two children, been divorced, and twice excommunicated. The brief biography at the back of this book doesn't tell us in what order these assorted triumphs and disasters occurred, nor does it vouchsafe into what church he was originally ordained. This is a pity, because he assures us that God loves us but doesn't indicate which god. Jehovah doesn't love us and has said so; I doubt that Allah loves us, but I won't pontificate on that theme because I don't want to have to go into hiding.

The main body of this book is divided into eight chapters; four are the stories of homosexual men who have confronted the laws of their country, and four are about lesbians who have adopted a similarly defiant stance. All these tales make fascinating, sometimes emotive reading. The murder of Harvey Milk is described again but, however often it is repeated, it remains a drama that evokes amazement and grief.

When I was young, my egotism prompted me to think of my cross as being heavier to carry than anybody else's, but, reading this book, I have become aware that being such a hopeless case had its advantages. From the moment I stepped out of my cradle, I knew what my problem was and so did everybody within a ten-mile radius. I lived in danger, but not in doubt. There is a story in *Profiles* of a Mrs Bottini, who married, produced two children and joined the National Organization for Women without being aware that she was a lesbian or that many of her friends had known this for years. Self-doubt nearly drove her insane.

The trouble with all the triumphs that the people mentioned in this book won, at such terrible risk to themselves, is that they are victories over the law rather than over life. This does not in any way lessen the admiration we feel for them, but it is necessary to reiterate over and over again that it is never the law that abruptly changes the world's attitudes: it is public opinion that very gradually modifies the law. The removal of a statute from a book does not make anybody's neighbours behave any more considerately. In England, my persecutors didn't care that I was illegal, nor even that I was immoral. They hated me because I was effeminate. A civic conscience and a sense of moral outrage are very rare but a feeling of revulsion against what seems unnatural is almost universal – no easier to eradicate than an inclination towards homosexuality.

*   *   *

The nicest letter of the week comes from Miss Liz Smith. It is a kind message written in the margin of a photocopy of her column in *Newsday* where she quotes a remark I made on Ronald Reagan the Younger's television show. I said that the way to improve gay relations with the straight world would be to refrain from talking about sex for a long time to come. She says that she absolutely cannot do this, and I accept that my proposal was unrealistic. When Mr Gandhi suggested that the way to decrease the alarming overpopulation of India was for married couples to practise abstinence, *Time* magazine said of this idea that it was 'long on logic, short on probability'. I am regretfully aware that the same criticism can be offered to me.

The nastiest letter comes from a gentleman in England whose signature I cannot read. I recently wrote an article denouncing the evils of 'outing' for the London *Evening Standard*. This almost illegible epistle is a reply, but says nothing about outing. Instead, it vents the writer's fury on my use of the word 'gay' for my own 'perverted and depraved use', and tries to give buggery a bad name, reminding me that it was made illegal in 1533.

I answer almost all correspondence – even the most hostile – and, in this case, I suppose I ought to point out to this indignant gentleman that many homosexual men do not indulge in this particular form of copulation. (In her very explicit book, *The Love Quest*, Felicity Mason says that none of her homosexual lovers ever tried it on her, but that several straight men made the attempt.) Somehow, I haven't the energy for trying to acquire another 'pen foe'.

Autumn

*

*Perhaps I should buy a lamp and stand on a rock
in New York harbour*

The pace of life in the smiling and nodding racket quickens. It is now rumoured that *Resident Alien* will open in Manhattan on 18 October. This is the movie by Mr Nossiter in which I wander round the streets saying anything that comes into my head to anyone who will listen. It will be shown at the Angelika Cinema. This location places it in a twilight zone between unabashed festival material and genuine entertainment. Naturally, the attempt to shift the picture's status involves promotion, and promotion involves visits at dusk to such never-before-heard-of towns as Madison in New Jersey.

Last Monday and Tuesday, an extremely courageous gentleman called Professor Rose, who presides over something called Sneak Preview Symposium, arranged for *Resident Alien* to be shown at his local cinema and persuaded his nephew to bring me, Mr Nossiter, and one of the film's publicists out of New York into an altered state. These circumstances led me to expect an audience consisting entirely of students. I was wrong. The auditorium contained people of all ages and sexes. Sad to say, the space was not quite full. Apparently, some members of the audience departed in indignation. (One woman, as she left, was heard to hiss, 'Did you see him? He hasn't changed his clothes since the film was made!') Even those who remained were outspoken – to say the least. Someone began her remarks with the words, 'I thought the least boring part was . . .'

The most important thing I learned from this entire occasion was that I am becoming deaf. Doubtless my friends have been aware of my infirmity for some time; I hadn't noticed. I can hear easily what is said close at hand, but even in that medium-sized auditorium every question had to be relayed to me by the Professor. I shall be sorry when this manifestation of my decline is complete. I don't mind not seeing much, but I like to hear everything except music. Words are my staple diet.

The letter of the week comes from someone who is about to visit a city in Germany with his parents so that they can be united by the university with the students with whom they worked before 1939 when they left – hurriedly. Never before, as far as I know, has any country made a public act of contrition for the past sins of its rulers. It is a truly commendable civic gesture, but I cannot help adding that I hope I shall never be brought face to face with any of the little swine who made my life such hell when I was at school.

I know that the British press complains that I am boring on the subject of the joys of living in America and the kindness of its inhabitants, but I persist in my folly by recounting the following episode.

Recently, when I boarded a Third Avenue bus, I found a newspaper lying on an otherwise empty seat. Immediately I scrabbled through its pages to find the crossword puzzle, which I carefully tore out and put in my pocket. Seeing me do this, a total stranger seated on the other side of the bus, without uttering a word, removed the puzzle from his paper and handed it to me. Greater love hath no man than that he lay down his crossword for a friend.

People used for ever to be asking me, 'Isn't there *anything* in England that you miss?' I could tell from the pleading tone in their voices that they wished me to have paid a high price for my present contentment, and it was with great reluctance that I said,

'No.' Now I have thought of a way to gratify their lust for the sorrows of others. There is one small disadvantage to living in America. When real winter arrives, the radiators of Manhattan begin to clank and hiss and tenants know that happiness – or, at least, heat – is on the way, but at this time of year while in the street it is still warm, indoors it is cool – occasionally too cool. I have a fair – nay, an indulgent – landlord, but there is not much we can do about this predicament. On the days when I remain at home from dawn till dusk and beyond, I do not like to sit around fully dressed; I like to loll about in a filthy dressing gown. It is more comfortable, and minimizes the wear and tear on my few 'going-out' clothes.

This quandary does not only occur in humble dwellings on the Lower East Side. When I first arrived from the other side of the globe to take up permanent residence here, I was compelled to throw myself on the mercy of a gentleman who lived in splendour on East 39th Street. Even there, the only solution to the problem of autumn was to light the gas cooker, leave the oven door open, and sit before it in a curious, hothouse atmosphere.

In England, however lowly my station in life became, in my bed-sitter I always had a tiny, asthmatic gas fire to which I could run home and by which I could crouch until I was warm. When I ask Americans why there are no gas fires in New York, they reply in shocked voices, 'Good heavens! Think of the explosions!' But many people have gas cookers. What is the difference in respect of their potential danger? The mystery remains, and I remain curled up over my typewriter, cocooned in a blanket with only my claws sticking out, like a large mole. Of course, I could live in San Diego, where the weather is always a cool summer, but then I wouldn't be in a position to rule the world, should the opportunity arise.

I have had a week in the eye of the hurricane of promotion. I have spent a lot of time lurking in my room and a little in neighbouring restaurants welcoming visitors from England. Perhaps I should buy a lamp and stand on a rock in New York harbour.

I have also been answering a spate of letters from Britain. The strangest of these comes from a woman who first wrote to me more than two years after one of my last-ever performances in London. The reason for that epistle is no longer clear in my mind, but I think that my audience had asked my opinion of suicide and that I had praised it. My correspondent had just rescued her daughter from a suicide attempt and was disturbed by this opinion. I replied that I realized that the mother could not have done otherwise than she did (it would have been illegal), but I warned her that she might now be blamed by her daughter for every humiliation that the young woman suffered in the future. The mother showed my letter to a friend who wrote consoling her and saying that I was cruel. What else could he say?`

Now, all these long, dark years later, she has sent me pictures of her house and her daughter with copies of my letter and the one from her friend. What can this mean? If her daughter's attempt to take her own life was a bid for attention, I cannot help being revolted. If it was a sincere act of desperation, and she is glad to have been restored to life, I am delighted for everyone concerned, but I am also quite bewildered. The girl must have summoned every ounce of her courage to deal once and for all with the miseries of the future, and is now once again faced with them.

The entire incident is quite extraordinary. Firstly, the mother must keep photostats of all her correspondence – even from total strangers. Secondly, and odder still, she must subscribe to the D.H. Lawrence notion that life is wonderful whatever happens. This is a fallacy that misdirects the behaviour of a lot of people – particularly anti-abortionists, although we all know that, if we are born to mothers who adore us, we may still not have a happy life. If our parents never stop reminding us that they never wanted us in the first place, we are in for a rotten time. How can anyone wish to make abortion difficult to obtain? Television shows us these publicity fiends abandoning every vestige of dignity by lying, like Arctic seals, on the pavement in front of family planning clinics, while on the same programme we are told that a garbage collector has found a baby a few hours old in a carrier bag in a dim alley.

I know that the expression of these views leads to the question of why I did not dispose of my useless self years ago. The answer is that I'm a sissy.

I went last week to New York University on Broadway. I must have passed this edifice many times, but have never noticed it. I have to say that it looks nothing like a venerable seat of learning. In England, education, which had once been decently confined, spread like a disease throughout the land. Universities sprang up in various provincial cities. Because their architecture lacked the Gothic dignity of Oxford and Cambridge they were contemptuously termed 'redbrick', and their teaching was assumed to be utilitarian rather than gloriously useless. In America, universities are evidently built of concrete, steel, and glass to indicate that they offer specifically New World, definitely twentieth-century knowledge. They even teach movie-making.

The interior of NYU is made entirely of wood with not an ink stain in sight; it looks like one vast Black & Decker project. While we sat on tubular steel chairs waiting to enter the college screening room, several young ladies passed us wearing kinky shoes and carrying gilt-tipped spears. Perhaps they were on their way to rehearsing as extras in an Equal Rights production of one of Mr Shakespeare's plays – possibly called *Henrietta the Fourth*.

In the screening room, unlike the audience to whom I spoke in Madison, there were no real people – only students, mostly male. They were either easy to entertain or, as I have found elsewhere in America, extremely polite. They did not have to be coaxed into speaking, and all their questions were technical – how long had it taken to make the film *Resident Alien*, for example. There were no questions about my life. From this I conclude that no NYU student is gay.

* * *

There is one remark which, in recent years, has been uttered by my audiences with noticeable frequency: 'Is there anyone that you particularly admire?' I have not yet found the right codified response. The expression 'role model' is comparatively new to me. In my earlier years there arose public icons, such as Mr Lindbergh, but I do not recall any exhortations from my elders to emulate such men. Perhaps such admonitions were uttered, but in my case they fell on deaf ears. Fate does not permit far-out homosexual men like me to indulge in such wishful thinking. We do not have ambitions; we have only fantasies. Like all the campy little creatures with whom I 'hung out' in my twenties, I lived in a swoon about one female movie star after another, but I never seriously expected to become like one of them, nor could I hope to reap rewards such as theirs. It may be for this reason that, while in an abstract way I greatly admire certain noble, courageous, or clever deeds, I do not seem to have much capacity for hero-worship. I hope this does not betoken any meanness of spirit. For me to want to be like some famous sportsman, some renowned philanthropist, or even some great artist would be living beyond my income of dreams.

Now I am back on the treadmill, flying from one extreme to another. On Monday, in the black of night, I was taken to the home of NBC, an impressive building in the middle of New Jersey. There I was interviewed by a Mr Matson, a gentleman of flawless respectability, for a programme called *The Real Story*. Although unaccustomed to reality in any form, I did my best to answer the usual questions in the usual way. On Tuesday, in pouring rain, I went to an office on West 26th Street, where I was interrogated by Mr Lou Maletta, whom I have met before at a different address. His fortunes have evidently improved since then. Last time we were together, we occupied a space so constricted that if I leaned forward for dramatic emphasis, I went out of focus. Mr Maletta is perfecting his image. He now has a Texan straw hat, which he wears at all times, and on this occasion was wearing black trousers so close-fitting that it was possible to see what he was thinking, brigand's boots, and a Mexican moustache. Being interviewed by him could almost be described as a sensuous experience.

On the evening of the same day, *Resident Alien* was shown at the Archives, which is a hostel for homeless movies on East Second Street. Among the audience were my favourite journalist, Liz Smith, and the movie actress, Miss Hutton, who arrived wearing a Columbo raincoat and pre-ruined jeans and swathed in an aura of reckless beauty.

The worst is over. At least, I think it is. For a while, the journeys became ever more circuitous; the limousines, longer; the interviews, more repetitive; and the parties, noisier. But, at last, two performances of *Resident Alien* have been given to the world – or at least, at the Angelika Cinema. The film is now on its own: no more publicity can alter its fate. For the director's sake, I wish this venture well, but for myself, I am inevitably somewhat blasé about its chances of making money or bringing anybody fame. Because of my great age, my future is now (if it hasn't already passed).

I have been interviewed by a Mr Castro for *People* magazine. I was somewhat apprehensive about this meeting because some years ago, for the same periodical, a young lady had photographed me and that occasion had turned out to be quite an ordeal. I had gone to a vast room, on one wall of which a huge landscape had been painted. There I was divested of my jacket which was promptly slit down the back so that two enormous white feathered wings could be attached to my rib cage through the opening. Thus equipped, I sat for about three hours in a nest of surgical cotton, moving my arms this way and that like a Hindu idol. Why the young woman didn't take any old pictures of me and paint the wings and sky around the image, I shall never know. I don't think she wanted her work to be simple: I suspect she wished it to be expensive.

My more recent encounter with a member of the staff of *People* magazine was painless – better than that, worthwhile: I was given lunch.

Even on the very day of *Resident Alien*'s release, I was sent to Washington (without the faintest hope of becoming President). There I was questioned for a television programme called *Nightwatch*. Nearly all interviews consist largely of an attempt to present my early life as a perfumed fist being shaken in the face of British narrow-mindedness – an interpretation which I always try to correct by explaining that in fact I was a helpless victim of my nature pleading with the world to forgive my difference from it. The only new subject introduced into more recent discussions is the announcement by certain doctors that the brains of homosexual men are in some way physically female. I take this discovery very calmly; I am quite prepared to accept that there is something weird about every cell in my body – let alone about what little grey matter is in my skull. (Will it now be revealed that there is something male about the brain structure of lesbians?)

I do not scour each day's papers and magazines for reviews of any of my performances, but, if people send them to me, I read them carefully. I know that all public rebuttal of adverse criticism is undignified – not to mention useless, but I would like to express a faint bewilderment at the often-voiced description of me as 'opaque'. As far as I know, I have never given an evasive reply to any question about my ideas or events in my life. My responses are aphoristic, not in order to conceal my meaning, but because they have been made so often that they have become crystallized – if not fossilized. Criticism of *Resident Alien* seems to be in the same vein; it is said to reveal nothing new about me. How can it? It is sometimes compared unfavourably with *The Naked Civil Servant*. That earlier television play was completed when I was already sixty-six – long past the age when I could be overtaken by any major change other than decay. It was never my place to ask Mr Nossiter what his intention was in making this film. I merely presumed it was an attempt to depict my life in America, to show how far it has fulfilled my dream of it, and to allow some denizens of the Lower East Side to express their opinions of me.

I have known for some months that, at the very end of October, I would be sent to St Paul to speak on the subject of ageing to whomsoever in that city's gay population would listen. I had no idea what it was hoped that I would say, but I thought that, if my powers of improvisation failed, fate would intervene on my behalf.

I rose before dawn last Thursday in order to complete the rituals of reconstructing myself without undue haste, packed a hold-all that RSVP Cruises gave me in the happy time when I worked for them, and left the house as a grey day was breaking over Manhattan. Taxis are more numerous in New York than in any other city in the world; on this, as on other occasions, I had no difficulty in finding one. I arrived at La Guardia and in Minnesota at the scheduled times. I'd 'done' Minneapolis (as touring actors say) in 1986. Now, as then, Mr Willkie (whose grandfather had been the Republican candidate for President in 1940) met me at the airport and allowed me to stay in his home. As we walked to his car, I remarked, with a jolly laugh, that I had half-expected it to be snowing, and, indeed, I saw two or three flakes frolicking in the breeze. By the time we were well on our way into the city, it had begun to rain.

As night fell over St Paul, so did the snow. At home, we started to listen to the frequent weather reports – something that in New York I try to avoid doing. News reached us every few hours throughout the evening warning motorists that, by morning, the snow might be twelve inches deep. This prophecy was fulfilled. The university was shut and Friday's gathering of all the ancient homosexuals of Minneapolis was cancelled. All during Friday and Saturday, the storm raged and the news became ever more disastrous. In spite of this, I went to a bookshop called A Brother's Touch, where a clamorous crowd of about six customers arrived to receive my autograph.

From the bookshop, I was taken to call on a Professor and

Mrs White. But this time the snow had to be shovelled from the sidewalk before I could attempt to reach their house, and I had almost to be carried everywhere. I was amazed by the patience of my escort. Our hosts fed us with gingerbread and we talked of this and that – chiefly of ageing. Then we went to a huge hotel where the hardiest members of the gay community gathered for a drink, but by then all attempts to organize a public meeting had been abandoned.

On Sunday evening, Mr Willkie gave a party at which we ate, drank, and discussed assorted gay issues. I received the impression that the homosexuals of Minnesota are in favour of the separate-but-equal solution to their problems. Mr Willkie's 'constant companion' recalled that I had once declared that, if Mr Bush announced that he was converting Indiana into a reservation for homosexual people and that we must all go and live there, I would burst into tears. It is true that I did make this statement: I would feel that I was being starved of reality. If I think about my life, I see it as a slow journey from the outer suburbs of ostracism almost to the heart of the world – assuming it has a heart. I would not wish to be shunted into a siding. Most of the guests did not share this view, but it was a really enjoyable evening at which people talked instead of merely chatting.

In a way, the terrible weather was a blessing, because I have no idea what I could have said about old age. Mrs White, the ginger-bread lady, said she didn't mind ageing, but did not want to be old. She deferred this inevitable state by never looking back, on the same principle, presumably, that prompts anyone walking along a girder twenty floors above the ground not to look down. Personally, I look neither forward, where there is doubt, nor back-ward, where there is regret; I look inward and ask myself not if there is anything out in the world that I want and had better grab quickly before nightfall, but whether there is anything inside me that I have not yet unpacked. I want to be certain that, before I fold my hands and step into my coffin, what little I can do and say and be is completed.

Back in the real world, the routines of my life quickly engulfed me. A small television crew arrived from England to photograph me for the BBC, of all people! Apparently, a whole week of their television time is to be devoted to the subject of homosexuality.

The mind boggles.

It seems that I owe the women of America an apology. I have just received from a friend in Key West a letter reproving me for something I wrote last month concerning the Judge Thomas scandal. My correspondent's opinion is couched in phrases of such extreme indignation that I became quite frightened when I read them. I had written that I was suspicious of Anita Hill's accusations firstly because they were dredged up from the past after all other attempts to prevent the judge's nomination had failed, and secondly, because she was so obviously in full control of herself and her circumstances that it seemed unlikely that she could have found no tactful way of side-stepping, if not actually silencing, his suggestive remarks. My friend tells me that, however carefully she had tried to deal with that situation, she would have been dismissed without a reference. He adds that, though never sexually harassed, he has been repeatedly abused and humiliated by his employers.

I'm stunned. In all the long dark years that I lived in England, though the office boys giggled whenever and wherever I appeared, and though of course I was underpaid, I was never insulted or bullied by my superior in any job. Furthermore, though I knew any number of women who told me their troubles (sometimes in squalid detail), not one of them ever recounted being subjected to grossly degrading treatment by male co-workers. As for an English high court judge mentioning his sexual organs to anyone – even to God – the idea is unthinkable. I am sure that the attitude of such an august personage towards his penis would have been similar to the response in England to the question, 'Do you have a television set?' There would be a reluctant admission: 'I do have one, but of course I never look at it.'

Can it be that there are some things better managed in Britain than over here?

I have been taken to Film Forum to see a three-dimensional version of Bugs Bunny and *Dial M for Murder*. For any picture to profit from an extra dimension, it would have to be full of violent movement. To Mr Hitchcock's very neat melodrama, it adds nothing, but it didn't prevent it from remaining a very enjoyable movie. As my companion remarked, *Dial M* is hardly more than a photographed play. Apart from a few glimpses of the streets in front of Mr Milland's London house, all the action takes place in his living room. When I first saw it many years ago (in two dimensions), I accepted it all without question. Now the dialogue seems threadbare and the acting almost comically perfunctory. Moreover, the extreme unlikelihood of a convicted murderess being allowed out of prison even for a moment is a quite gratuitous addition to the story's long list of improbabilities. The trap set for Mr Milland would have worked just as well without her being present to watch it.

I have been to Atlanta, a city of which I already had happy memories. The first time I was asked to go to Georgia was so that I could attend a book signing. When I told the publicity lady for that project that I thought Atlanta had been burned down, she said, 'Well, we built it up again, just for you,' and it looked just as though they had. Every object, every building, every street that met the eye looked brand-new.

On my second visit, I really lived a little while: I met Miss Rosemary Clooney. She was performing at what, in the early 1930s, had been one of Mr Fox's cinemas, an edifice so large that its foyer was as big as the average modern movie house. What a happy era Miss Clooney's name recalls! She sang as though she understood and cared what the words of her songs meant.

On this visit, I seemed to be in an entirely different part of town. I stayed at the Wyndham Hotel, from the front windows of which it was possible to see but fifty yards away Mrs *Gone-with-the-Wind* Mitchell's home, an odd little house with a steeply sloping roof and a lot of gables.

Atlanta seems to have become publicity mad. Though it was on Sunday that I arrived, within an hour a young man was interviewing me; someone else appeared at three, and a third person at half past five. In the evening I was dined by a Mr Moon (humorously called Sunny) of the *Midtown Times*, whom I had met on an earlier sojourn in the city. The next day, there were more interviews, two of them taking place more or less simultaneously. A Mr Hopgood arrived at the same time that a young woman called to take me to a television station to be questioned by an ex-beauty queen. I followed my escort in Mr Hopgood's car. He held his tape recorder in one hand and the steering wheel with the other, but we came to no harm.

My aversion to culture is at least as strong as that of Marshal Goering. It was, therefore, with many a furtive glance to left and right that I entered the building on West 58th Street that is the self-proclaimed home of WNET, Channel 13. I was there at the request of Mrs Michael York, who had included a photograph of me in her book, *Going Strong*, to take part in a television programme ruled by a Mr Rose. In the green room, I found Kitty Carlisle, whose name is etched for ever on my memory because of a remark she made to me many years ago. I had said that I thought all Mr Williams' plays were about how awful it is to be a woman, to which she replied, 'I think they are about how awful it was to be Tennessee Williams.'

We were soon joined by a lawyer whose name I have forgotten, but, like Miss Carlisle, he was engaged in what used to be called good works and on a world scale. I couldn't help wondering how on earth I came to be co-starred with them. They are devoting their time and energy to unceasing selfless activity: I retired at birth. Indeed, I drink daily from that deep well that people like them have dug. They are striving for a better world: I am it. What do you suppose they thought when brought face to face with a living example of the result of their handiwork?

I try to prevent traditions and even habits from creeping into my way of life, but I do not entirely succeed. Every Thanksgiving Day for at least the past five years, I have been a guest at the New Jersey home of my friend's family. His uncle collects me from Manhattan and returns me. It is a very convivial occasion; the hospitality has to be consumed to be believed. I have a wonderful time, but I ought not to indulge myself in this way; I do not have the right. Not only am I not a member of this family but I am not even an American. Historically speaking, I have nothing for which to do a thanksgiving; I am only English and should, on this day, be sitting in my room doing penance for not having beheaded Charles I sooner.

There is also another, darker tradition in my life which recurs inevitably, but at more widely spaced, less regular intervals. This is a sickness which has no cause, no name, and no cure. Its symptoms are a loss of temperature, a loss of appetite, a loss of energy, and finally, a loss of hope. Once it begins, I can only wait for this malady to pass and, so far, it always has.

This year, both these traditions, the one so gay, the other so grim, occurred more or less simultaneously. On the return journey from Port Monmouth, though swaddled in a woolly overcoat and wedged cosily with four other people into a small car, I began to feel chilly. By the time I reached my front door, I was shivering so convulsively that I could hardly insert my latch-key into the lock. I almost fainted clambering up the stairs to my room and, once there, I sat for hours without removing my outer garments, shuddering.

Since then I have done almost nothing until last Sunday, when I was forced out into a mournful fringe of rain to meet a very friendly middle-aged couple who have caught glimpses of me on their television set during the BBC's unprecedented week of 'gay' programmes. (As Mr Clary remarked when he was there, 'In

England, you're much more likely to be beaten up on the street, but on the telly you can *say* anything.') Needless to say, my new acquaintances adore Mr Clary. While I lived in Britain, if I had met these two charming people in public, I would have been terrified of them, but now, because television has spun this sparkling web of amity across the whole world, I am able to talk to them and others like them without hesitation, without formality, and without reservation. I guess that I am the person who has profited more from the invention of television than anybody else.

Never again should anyone speak ill of the United States Postal Service. Someone in Birmingham, England, sent me a letter in an envelope, on the front of which were only the words, 'Quentin Crisp, New York, America,' and, on the back, apologies to the mailman and a plea begging him to find me.

He did.

Winter

*

All of society's outsiders must live in big cities

I have been a guest at a party of quite daunting elegance given by a Mr Woolley in his home on the upper reaches of Fifth Avenue. (Even Miss Fran Lebowitz was formally attired.) I sat with Miss Smith, who, having seen my room in *Resident Alien*, expressed concern for my financial status. She must be the only gossip writer in the world interested in the welfare of her victims, as opposed to wheeling above their heads waiting for disaster to overtake them. I also spent time with a young man who scolded me for saying that I was eagerly awaiting my death. Was I bored, he wanted to know. My answer is an emphatic NO: the kindness and hospitality of Americans ensures that I am never bored, but, because of my great age, I am occasionally exhausted.

At the beginning of last week, my unnamed illness re-recurred. I returned home one evening stricken by the intense cold and was just about to give way to a fit of vomiting when my telephone rang. I answered my caller in a strangulated voice which caused him to remark that I sounded different. I replied, 'Things are bad at the moment, please call me another time.' 'What's the matter?' he asked, but I could only murmur, 'Another time,' and rang off. My friend's reaction to this admittedly unusual response was to telephone his uncle, who lives in Manhattan, the paramedics, and the New York Police Department. The uncle replied at once, but I am happy to report that no one else did. If they had been able to enter the house, they would have discovered me clad only in confusion, trying to clean up the mess

I had made of myself and my room by being unable to reach the bathroom in time.

The moral in this incident seems to be that it is unwise to present to the world a façade of monumental imperturbability, because the effects are so disastrous if it ever collapses.

Another slight but strange incident occurred when I was visiting Jack Eric Williams. I forgot to wear my monocle with the result that, when I entered the apartment building where he lives, I could not read the numerals and letters engraved on the strip of metal beside the huge array of bells. As I was in New York, I imagined that all I needed to do was to go back into the street and ask the first stranger passing by to enter the building with me and read me the numbers. I happened upon a young woman. When, holding the street doors open, I explained my predicament, she declined to help me, saying, 'Oh no, I couldn't come in. I'm too nervous.' I repeated that I only wanted her to read some numbers, but she still hesitated. At that moment, two inmates of the apartment house emerged and I was able to dart forward before the inner doors closed. As I did so, I called back, 'I'm sorry I frightened you,' and, just before the doors shut, I heard her reply, 'I'm sorry I was nervous.' This young woman has the distinction of being the only uncooperative person in the entire United States.

My faith in the American character, shattered last week by the young woman who refused to help me read the numbers of the bells in a dim apartment building, has been restored. On Christmas Eve, I went to our local post office to collect four parcels that the postman had been unable to deliver at our house because there are no front door bells. One of these gifts was so large that it was in a Santa Claus kind of sack. Thoroughly dismayed, I went out into Fourth Avenue to try to persuade a taxi driver to wait while I carried all these packages on to the sidewalk. There I found an unknown young man, who had observed my predicament, waiting to assist me. Without his help, I would never have been able to transport all this load of Yuletide generosity home.

The most mysterious of these gifts turned out to be a book called *A Poet Could Not But Be Gay*, the second instalment of an ongoing autobiography by Mr James Kirkup, the first part of which was called *I, of All People*. The very title of this new volume is naughty. It is a quotation from poor Mr Wordsworth's all-too-well-known poem about daffodils and has absolutely nothing to do with the modern meaning of the word 'gay'. The contents of the book are less skittish; in fact, they are largely tragic, but they are fascinating.

There is an unalterable law that states that all of society's outsiders must live in big cities and Mr Kirkup knows this. Nevertheless, when this section of his life story begins, he is staying with his parents in Corsham, an unknown village in the west of England. He feels that the local police are watching him and, as his paranoia increases, he begins to think that he is under the surveillance of MI5 and even the CIA. He is also aware that his mother and father are suffering silently because of his eccentricities, but does not know until after they are dead that they actually received poisonous letters about their son. (To my surprise, he expresses no amazement that they kept these threatening missives.)

It was quite inevitable that he would become an object of public interest and even public scorn. He wore make-up (indeed, he describes himself as an obsessive *maquilleur*), and once peroxided his already fair hair until most of it fell out. Furthermore, his chosen profession was teaching, where he was a figure of fun to his students who were at an age when cruelty is rampant. In desperation, he went to Sweden, which to my surprise he enjoyed, and to Spain, where he was almost as frightened of the authorities as he had been of the British constabulary. Apparently, in the 1950s, when Mr Franco and the Pope jointly ruled this country, deviancy of any sort was forbidden. In spite of this, his descriptions of Spain are marvellous.

Mr Kirkup is a poet. I write these words in very small print because I know that a poet is a terrible thing to happen to anybody. Even Mr Kirkup himself didn't like poets and shunned literary cliques; he didn't much like people of any kind. He was by nature a loner, but he keenly felt his loneliness: what he wanted was what I once called 'the great dark man', and what he terms 'someone to watch over me'. Naturally, this person he never found, but he did meet an American student with whom he at first had a weird relationship in which they wrote poetry together, and later a torrid affair.

To me the only weakness of this fascinating book is that several of the author's poems are inserted into the text. They become an interruption because we read verse in a different way, at a different pace from prose.

On Christmas Day I became eighty-three, but managed to ignore the fact by visiting friends and eating other people's food. On New Year's Eve my energies deserted me and, though I received two very attractive invitations, I hid and read a novel called *Gaijin on the Ginza* by our Mr Kirkup. It is not about the intermittent quest for love, but about the incessant search for sexual gratification. It makes it seem that all Japanese young men are frustrated and that almost all will respond to overtures from whatever direction. Another distinction is that this tale is not tragicomic: it is hilarious.

Mr Kirkup has lived for many long, dark years in Japan and is rumoured to prefer it to England, which is natural enough, but also to everywhere else, which is surprising. In spite of this preference, this book makes fun of every aspect of Japanese life – the universal black clothing, the conventionality, the perpetual bowing (even to invisible listeners at the other end of telephone wires), the social hypocrisy, and the ingrained insularity. He tells us that the Japanese, in spite of all their politeness to them, will never accept foreigners as their equals. If this book is ever translated into Japanese, Mr Kirkup will be deported.

The story tells of a middle-aged and excruciatingly campy English teacher, who wears monocles tinted to match his outfits, and of his newly acquired assistant, who is a young Diana Dors type of English girl with no experience of teaching and no aptitude for it. They spend most of their time staring at the front of young men's trousers. In the end, the man is murdered by one of his pick-ups, who feels that he has been underpaid for his services, and almost everybody else dies of AIDS. I felt that this conclusion was a bit glib, but everything that happens on the way there, though extremely bawdy, is great fun.

I have had lunch with two charming young women who are working for an English movie company which is planning to produce a film version of *Orlando*, Mrs Woolf's most highbrow novel. One of these ladies is a dress designer, and the other is a wiggist. We all came back to my room so that they could measure me for one of those rigid costumes with a pointed bodice reaching down as far as you-know-what and a bright orange wig so that I can appear in this production as Elizabeth I. We all agreed that there is no portrait in existence showing Miss Tudor wearing any such highly coloured contraption on her head, but, in the movie industry, this tradition persists. Who am I to protest?

If this improbable venture ever actually comes to pass, I will be transported to Amsterdam for two weeks of next month. There is a Quentin Hotel in that notorious city. On seeing the same, a friend of mine entered the lobby and asked the proprietress if the establishment was so called in honour of me, to which they replied, 'But of course.' Whether or not I shall be allowed time to visit this place I have no idea.

My hostility to culture is at its fiercest in the matter of music because music is obtrusive – even, on occasion, inescapable; my aversion is at its mildest concerning literature, which is virtually invisible. The visual arts lie somewhere in between these two extremes; they can be taken or left. For the most part, I leave them.

Mr Cocteau once said that pictures are only the perspiration that the artist flings off while taking his exercise, and that what matters is what exercise he takes. I agree. I once shocked a teacher at the Royal College of Art by telling his students that the great painters of this century were Augustus John, Salvador Dali, David Hockney and Andy Warhol. Though of these only Mr Hockney is a great draughtsman, all these men are more famous than their work.

What a delightful hotel the Algonquin is! It is fourteen long, dark years since I stayed there, and Mr Ansbach, the owner, sat in the lobby with me and gave me glasses of port, but the staff always behaves as though it remembers me.

Last week I went there for breakfast with the gentleman who rules the display department of Paul Stuart and a charming young lady who seems more or less to rule the entire establishment. The Algonquin no longer serves creamed haddock and all those old-fashioned dishes that were available in the English country mansions featured in Mrs Christie's novels, but we ate a very pleasant meal during which my hosts talked about their advertising. Gradually, I began to realize that they wanted me to write some copy for their spring catalogue. When we were leaving, they presented me with a wooden star, though I doubt I'll ever be sheriff – even for the Lower East Side. I also dutifully took away with me samples of their previous advertisements, which I have since read, but they only convince me that this is work that I am totally unable to do. This is especially mortifying because, after breakfast, the display king was kind enough and brave enough to walk up Seventh Avenue with me in an arctic gale. I now realize that I am guilty of a crime that on the statute books will be called 'obtaining poached eggs under false pretences'.

My reason for travelling, in spite of the weather, to the upper reaches of Seventh Avenue was to undergo a medical examination at the hands of a Dr Benson on behalf of Adventure Pictures, the company that is proposing to make *Orlando*, the movie in which I will play Elizabeth I. When I was in Mr Sting's film, *The Bride*, no such ordeal was forced upon me. I mentioned to the good doctor that I had never before been medically examined, to which he replied, 'You're worth a lot of money' – and, after a slight pause – 'to somebody.' He then photographed my lungs, electrified my heart, extracted blood from my right arm and urine from my bladder, and told me my blood pressure was high. I was not surprised to hear this. My march along the freezing streets was enough to raise anyone's blood pressure. The last time that I was tested in that particular way was in Australia, when all the doctor said, in a gloomy voice, was 'It's better than mine.' What this verdict meant I was unable to judge.

Not long ago, I was asked if I would consent to appear on the cover of a dubious magazine. As it is my policy never to say no to anything, I agreed. I may now have to reconsider my policy, because on one very cold evening this week I had to endure the consequences of saying yes. I was taken by an unknown gentleman to a studio in the depths of the meat-marketing district. We arrived at about six o'clock, and were met by the owner of the place, a photographer, a make-up artist, and sundry helpers. I reckon that the effort to reconstruct my face took about an hour, during which time a huge roll of green paper was hung against one wall and spread across part of the floor. When it was deemed that nothing more could be done to humanize me, I was taken into a lavatory where I squeezed the lower half of my body into a pair of black panty hose and a pair of skin-tight black trousers. I was relieved that an attempt to force my upper half into a frilly blouse was abandoned. Then, with my trousers and my dim grey long-johns over my arm, I returned to the photographic area, where I was swathed in a mock fur stole, lined with purple fabric, and as big as a king-sized bedspread, and a weird, white woolly hat shaped like a chamber pot was placed on my head. There was even an effort made to cram my bunioned feet into a pair of black glacé shoes with two-inch-thick platforms and six-inch heels, but when it was discovered that I was unable to stand in them, this idea was abandoned. Halfway through the proceedings, it was decided that I should stand and that two unfortunate young men should be compelled to strip and stand on each side of me to support me. Their services were really needed, as the entire session lasted nearly four hours and towards the end I was ready to collapse. Everybody was extremely kind; someone fetched beer and food to sustain me, and an electric fire was found to warm me, but nothing could prevent the evening from being an ordeal only slightly less exhausting than being in a movie. Recently, Miss Lauren Hutton asked me why I didn't try to find work as a photographic model. They earn thousands of dollars a day, she informed me. I know why.

Not only does it seem likely that I will play the part of Elizabeth I in a highbrow movie, but even in real life I am beginning to resemble English royalty in that, in recent years, I have celebrated my real birthday on Christmas Day quietly with friends who live on Fourth Street, and a state birthday whenever one of Manhattan's party-givers sees fit. Last Saturday I went to the Palladium for a public birthday. After a few drinks in an almost pitch-dark bar, the chosen descended into what the Baroness von Korber-Bernstein called 'the engine room'. There I was lavishly wined and dined and given a huge birthday cake while a stand-in for Miss Monroe sang 'Happy Birthday' in an appropriately breathy, last-gasp voice.

Even better, I was seated next to the wonderful Miss Sylvia Miles, who first commanded our attention on-screen in *Midnight Cowboy*, when she refused to believe that Mr Voight seriously expected *her* to give *him* money, and of whom Mr Warhol once said, referring to her awesome social stamina, 'She would go to the opening of an envelope.'

The only reason why I didn't ask my host to send invitations to everybody who knows me was that I could not tell and did not like to ask if all the guests had been charged for admission. Even I, egomaniac that I am, haven't the nerve to ask anyone to part with good money for the doubtful privilege of dining with me.

Now that I celebrate my birthday on several occasions round

this time of year, I receive a large number of well-wishing letters for which I am sincerely grateful. In the longer letters from total strangers, there often occurs the question, 'Who influenced you?' and, occasionally, 'What books influenced you?' To these queries I am always at a loss for a satisfactory answer. If anyone shaped my character, I suppose it was my parents – particularly my mother – and, regretfully, I admit that, because of them, I am invincibly middle-class. Apart from them, I can't think that my destiny was formed by anything but bad luck. I endured a life which offered very few options.

To speak in broader terms, the words 'role model' are not in general use in England; they express a purely American notion. As I see it, if a boy wishes to emulate Babe Ruth, he is already like Babe Ruth. All he needs is the stamina and the luck. I have admired many people, but know that I have no hope of resembling any of them or of ever receiving the rewards that they enjoyed. I am too far removed from the human arena.

On Monday evening, I went to The Book Friend's Café, on West 18th Street. I had been there once before with some friends from Dayton, so I was not frightened by the somewhat arty name of the place. There is no need to look at the books. Customers are allowed to treat the establishment entirely as a restaurant. It serves good, understandable food; that is to say that the chicken looks like chicken and has not been tortured by haute cuisine into resembling something else. Another advantage of eating there is that there is *no* music. The reason for my being there on this occasion was not so much to eat as to hear what a Mr Hoare had to say about his book, *Serious Pleasures*, which is a biography of Stephen Tennant, a famous English aesthete about whom all London gossiped when I was young. I was especially curious about the author because I had read the book and reviewed it, though I cannot now remember for what paper.

Before the lecture, Mr Hoare sat with me for a few minutes and thanked me for what I had written about his book. In appearance, he is a little like his subject, but without the languorous expression, the heavy make-up, or the pearls.

I am a great admirer of Mr Sean O'Casey. When I was about seventeen years of age, the Irish Players, whose stars were Sara Allgood and Maire O'Neill, arrived in London from the Abbey Theatre of Dublin to perform *The Plough and the Stars* and *Juno and the Paycock*. As the saying goes, they took London by storm. For weeks, theatre-goers talked about nothing else. At that time, acting in London was highly theatrical and the naturalism of the Irish Players was shattering, though I do not remember anyone discussing the contents of the dramas or arguing the rights and wrongs of Britain's occupation of Ireland. In *The Plough*, in my opinion Mr O'Casey's greatest work, when Miss O'Neill is shot, she puts her hand behind her back for a moment and then looks to see it covered with blood. ' 'Tis me own life blood streamin' out,' she gasps. This is the only time I can ever remember being so caught up in a play that I thought, 'She's dying,' and had to remind myself that she was only acting.

Mr Agate, the famous drama critic, could not make up his mind whether this play or *Saint Joan* was the masterpiece of the century. Their appeals couldn't be more different. Mr Shaw's play is a stimulating moral argument; Mr O'Casey's is a heart-rending document.

Though the programme sets the time of the play between 1880 and 1910, its action includes a glimpse of 'The Troubles', as they were called, in 1916, and we see the Dubliners being quelled by the British police, but this play is strictly about the life of Mr O'Casey and only marginally about the fate of Ireland. We see the playwright as a little boy with a troublesome eye disease (Mr Moyles), as a young man (Mr Fitzgerald), and in old age (Mr O'Neill). In the end they are all on stage at the same time in conversation with each other. This device gives the play a poetic and very moving unity.

While I was typing the last words of the above, an unknown

woman telephoned me to ask me for eighteen dollars and fifty cents. I told her to come to the front door, where I handed her a twenty-dollar bill. She thanked me and departed. As I walked back upstairs to my room, I wondered if I should hear from her again in a month or two. I misjudged her. Within two hours, an operator was asking me if I would pay for a call. I said, 'No.' A few minutes later, the unknown woman was telephoning me with another incomprehensible saga of misfortune. I refused to give her any more money. I hated myself for this, but I hated her even more. Since I came to America, she is the first person to drive me beyond the bounds of politeness.

Last Friday, with trembling feet, I made my way to the Warner Building in Rockefeller Plaza to record an assortment of English verses by various poets from Edward Lear to Edith Sitwell for a mad friend who teaches voice production to a heap of drama students in the middle of Kansas City. Of all the Englishmen living in America, I must be the one with the least resonant voice, but I was asked to do it and offered money, so I could hardly refuse.

Because it was a sunny day and because the entire assignment had taken only about a quarter of an hour, after it I walked all the way to The Book Friend's Café on West 18th Street to have lunch with the display king from Paul Stuart. It was foolish of me to undertake so long a journey on foot, because I arrived at my destination in a state of total moral and physical collapse. However, so kind are the people who rule this restaurant that they allowed me to loll about on a very comfortable sofa, fingering the pages of various antiquarian books, from half past eleven until high noon when my host arrived. When we had eaten some chicken pot pie, we went to the new cinema on West 19th Street to see *Final Analysis*. I have to confess that, owing to my marathon walk a few hours before, I fell asleep several times during the showing of this film, but even if I had been as watchful as an owl, I think I would still have found its story-line confusing. It concerns a psychoanalyst (Mr Gere) who probes the soul of a girl who is in a permanent rage with her more successful sister. This piques his curiosity and leads him to arrange a meeting with the sister (Miss Basinger), with whom he almost immediately begins an affair. She manages to weave into her conversation with him various psychological clues to her assumed dodgy mental condition that will make it possible for her to murder her husband and get away with it on a plea of temporary insanity. When he realizes that he is being used, he refuses to cooperate and she decides to murder him, too. Everybody ends up at the top of an extremely shaky lighthouse (don't ask me why), and only Mr Gere survives.

Final Analysis is the third in a series of movies about absolutely diabolical women. Miss Basinger, though she hasn't the frenzied look of Miss Close in *Fatal Attraction*, nor the demonic cunning of Miss DeMornay in *The Hand That Rocks the Cradle*, is perfectly adequate. Mr Gere is very good-looking – like a Chippendale stripper or like Errol Flynn with the mainspring gone – and his performance is quite satisfactory because this is one of those pictures where the plot is so elaborate that the function of the actors involved is to carry out the action rather than to reveal character. The only member of the cast who is outstanding is Mr David as a black detective who trusts absolutely nobody. I would recommend *Final Analysis* as a very pleasant waste of seven dollars and fifty cents.

The next day, like You-Know-Who, I rested, but on Sunday I went to Boston – again! This time it snowed, but at least there was no hurricane.

The purpose of this second excursion was the same as that of the first – to introduce beforehand and to try to justify afterwards two showings of *Resident Alien*. These took place in Brookline in an art house called The Coolidge, ruled by a Mr Kleiler, who positively despises movies made for the purpose of entertainment. He turned out to be a charming and generous host to me and to Mr Nossiter, the film's director, who travelled with me. I never had an unoccupied moment, and never walked anywhere.

The questions asked of me were all friendly, but more or less a matter of routine, except that one young man wanted to know what I would have done with my life if I had been under no obligation to earn money. I replied that I would never have gotten out of bed. Everybody seemed delighted with this notion.

1992

Spring

*

*People who are lonely are those who do not know what to
do with the time when they are alone*

To hell and back. On March 9th, I set out timorously for England;
I returned home in a state of total nervous and physical collapse
on the 24th. The purpose of this misguided journey halfway across
the globe was to make a minuscule appearance as Elizabeth I, in
a movie to be entitled *Orlando* and made from a novel of that
very name by the very Mrs Woolf of whom the Burtons were so
afraid. All her books were highbrow, and this was certainly the
most highbrow. It concerns a young man whom we first meet at
Hatfield House in the middle of Hertfordshire (where the young
Elizabeth spent much of her childhood), and who lived through
the centuries until the present day, incidentally changing his sex
on the way, sometime during the seventeen hundreds. This fantastic tale was said to be a tribute to Vita Sackville-West, with whom
prurient literary historians claim that Mrs Woolf conducted an
illicit liaison. (I, personally, don't think Mrs Woolf believed in
sex; she was too much of an aesthete.)

On arriving in London, I went to stay at the Chelsea Arts Club
where, at breakfast the next morning, everyone cried out in tones
of deepest reproach, 'Thought you were never coming back.' I was
truly ashamed, because a farewell party had been given for me
there two and a half years ago. I could only bow my head and
offer, as an extenuating circumstance, that I had returned for the
money.

After a day or two, during which I had been fitted for a dress
and a wig, Miss Tilda Swinton, the star of the film, arrived to

welcome me to England with a bouquet of roses and a gift. Her most recent role was that of Queen Isabella in *Edward II*, a film directed by Mr Jarman: we can therefore assume that she is accustomed to appearing in unabashed festival material and, indeed, she seems to prefer it to real movies.

Once my part in *Orlando* began in earnest, I left the club and moved to Bush Hall, a small hotel in Hatfield, so as not to rise at five in the morning on the days when work began at seven. There I was given a room so large that I could have a party for twenty people in it, and was treated with such deference that, on the occasion when I ate lunch there, the proprietor himself served me with his own two hands.

On my first day of work, I realized instantly that I was doomed to a life of agony. Two amazingly long-suffering dressers wedged me into a costume in which two padded rolls forming a kind of bustle, a hooped skirt, a quilted petticoat, another petticoat, and finally an outer skirt were all tied round my waist before I was laced into a corset so tight that it raised a blister on my stomach. Over all this, I wore a cloak that trailed the ground behind me and on which two elk-hounds and Miss Swinton occasionally stepped, causing me to utter a cry of apprehension and to totter about the lawn. Never in the history of dress design has so much glass been affixed to so many yards of tat.

Apart from all this, I was made up clown-white with a dusting of rouge on my cheeks and eyelids and clamped into a huge red wig at times surmounted by a tiara. Apparelled thus, before I could leave the trailer, called a 'relocatable', a gentleman, appropriately named Christian, had to hold up my skirts and, watching my feet, utter instructions such as 'One step down. Now the other leg. Right. You're on level ground.' Carrying all this haberdashery caused my back to ache ferociously, and that was before I had fallen back in a high chair so that my skull crashed against the opposite wall of the make-up room and my back muscles were stretched out of shape.

Sometimes I worked in one or the other of the vast rooms of

Hatfield House, sometimes in the grounds, and once, in the middle of the night, on a lake that was really more like a pond. For this scene, real men were employed to row a small boat back and forth several times while, in another boat, a charming young man called Mr Somerville sang in a falsetto voice a song telling the world that I was 'the fairest queen'. What he thought of this assignment I did not dare to enquire.

During this ordeal, Miss Potter, the director, Miss Swinton, the star, and everyone concerned were all most solicitous and kind, but I cannot deny that I am heartily glad that it is over.

Although I try never to read books, I am now perusing two concurrently, dipping into whichever happens to be on hand when a spare moment occurs. One of these is Mr Cocteau's diary, entitled (in translation) *Past Tense*, and the other is called *Final Exit*, by a Mr Humphry, a journalist who used to write for *The Sunday Times* in London and the *Los Angeles Times*, chiefly about civil liberties, racial integration, and voluntary euthanasia.

I have now forgotten who lent me the former of these two volumes, but doubtless he will reclaim it one fine day. It has a foreword by Mr Ned Rorem, which by itself is worth the price of the entire book. He was with Mr Cocteau at most eight times during the thirteen years of their acquaintance, but says that to meet him once was to know him. He writes, 'While you were with him, you were seemingly the sole beneficiary of his charitable flood of fire. I have known few people with such infectious charm. It may be opportunism, but it can't be faked, and it can't be bought.'

Final Exit is a handbook for anyone wishing to commit suicide. This was sent to me by a Mr Hofsess who, some years ago, came to New York, like the rest of us, in the hope of ruling the world. He stayed at least long enough to do most of the work on a book of mine, entitled *Manners From Heaven*. He then returned to Vancouver and, to my astonishment, has become king of the local branch of the Hemlock Society. He wishes me to write something about this book and I will. I have always liked death, especially other people's death, but have recently been contemplating my own with a certain amount of relish. Not long ago, during a television interview, I was asked if I was worried by the idea of mortality. I replied that I was not and added that next Tuesday would do fine for my own demise. This remark caused a concerned citizen to ask how I could possibly be so bored that I was eager to die. The question was natural because he was a young man. Ennui is the disease of youth. The prevailing malady of the old is fatigue. I have never been bored since I came to live in Manhattan, but, inevitably, I am gradually becoming permanently tired.

Even before senility set in, my views about death were sanguine, or, to put the matter another way, I have never shared the prevailing opinion that life is wonderful *come what may*. I have often been surprised when someone who has suffered a permanent injury in some disaster, says, 'I'm lucky to be alive.' If I were in a plane crash, for instance, and all my luggage – let alone one of my limbs – had sunk to the bottom of the Atlantic Ocean, I would not consider myself lucky to be alive. So, if told of someone's death, I will say, 'How terrible . . .' and look at the floor for an appropriate interval, but I can't really feel it is terrible because in my view death is the *least* awful thing that can happen to someone.

It is our bodies that want to live for ever, but surely we ought to be in control of our physical appetites. However, this is a state that it is easier to praise than to achieve. Nobody wants a violent or a painful death, and this is where Mr Humphry's book comes in so handy. It is totally unsentimental, absolutely free from religious bias, and admirably practical. My only divergence of opinion from that of the author is that I do not think that the relatives of the person committing suicide should be consulted or involved in any way. They may have something to gain from the proposed death and may therefore feel guilty. In all other respects, I am full of praise for *Final Exit* and for its author.

*   *   *

When not writing about death, I am still answering the mail that accumulated while I was in England. In it, the most interesting letter comes from a young woman with whom I had lunch recently, but not so recently that I can remember much about her. She complains that, although we were by ourselves and she was only the width of a dining-room table away from me, she felt that she was merely a member of an audience and that I was giving a performance rather than engaging in conversation. I am rebuked. I have often been guilty of assuming that, when strangers invite me to lunch or any other occasion, what they want is entertainment. It has always seemed unlikely that anyone would wish to confide in or even to impress a stranger, but this, of course, is nonsense. Many people can never reveal themselves to anyone who knows them, their friends or, worse, their parents. I am resolved henceforth to invite confidence or, at least, communication from everybody. The only demand made by strangers that I cannot satisfy is to utter confidences of my own; I don't have any. What you see is all there is. I dare not compare myself with Mr Cocteau in any way, but I would like to think that, as Mr Rorem said of him, to meet me once is to know me.

By a quirk of fate at least as strange as any of the plot of *Howards End*, on the same day that I saw Mrs Branagh in that film, I met her in real life.

Some time ago, when Mr Nossiter's movie about my life was being shown at the New School on West 12th Street, Professor Brown, who rules that establishment, invited me to attend the screening. I couldn't accept, but last Wednesday evening I was at last free. The occasion did not start well. A car arrived at Third Street promptly at half past seven but, when I jumped into it with alacrity, it transpired that the driver had no idea where he was to take me; neither had I. We drove round aimlessly until I persuaded him to telephone his employers and find out our true destination. When, finally, we arrived at the New School, mercifully a kind young woman was waiting for me and took me into a small room in which the professor's victims are stored until needed.

There I sat drinking coffee when suddenly Mrs Branagh arrived, and I learned that she was the professor's guest for the first half of the evening. I was able to listen to her interview, which I greatly enjoyed. She is much better looking in real life than in any of her films, and she was supremely natural, speaking to the professor rather than addressing the audience, and she was eager to be understood.

When my turn came, Professor Brown was very cosy, asking no difficult or embarrassing questions, but of course the presence of an audience went to my head and I tried to give a performance rather than hold a conversation, failing just where Mrs Branagh had succeeded. What a charming woman she is! On returning to the lurking area for my hat and coat, I found that she had left me a note apologizing for not staying to hear all I had to say. She had just arrived from England; therefore, though it was only nine in the evening to us, it was two in the morning to her.

When all the interviews were over, the professor took me and two of his handmaidens to supper at a nearby Italian restaurant. There it transpired that he was surprised that I had declined his previous invitation on the grounds that I was committed to a previous engagement. He said that Americans leave messages at restaurants saying that they will not be keeping their appointments. I would never dare to do that. What do I have to recommend me to the world other than that I keep my word?

This week's entry into my diary simply must begin with a vote of thanks to Miss Liz Smith, who is the only gossip writer in the world who retails remarks that encourage self-confidence rather than spread alarm and despondency. Perhaps she should be given a different title. Mary Renault would have dubbed her 'a praise singer'. She has now sent me a glowing review of *Resident Alien*, which I would otherwise never have seen. It appeared in a Washington newspaper, and was written by a Miss Kempley, to whom

I am also grateful. Naturally, most of the praise in her article is for Mr Nossiter, who made the film, but she is also nice to me. The only adjective that she applies to me with which I would disgree is the word 'lonely'. I live alone, but am glad to do so. To my mind, the people who are lonely are those who do not know what to do with the time when they are alone. From this problem I do not suffer. When I'm by myself, I do absolutely nothing, and O, the relief!

I have read a new biography of Jean Harlow, a copy of which was presented to me by the author, a Miss Golden, when I had lunch with her at our local diner. This book has been excellently produced by the Abbeville Press on paper almost as thick as cardboard and glossy enough to offset the beautiful photographs of the actress, her co-stars, members of her family, and her friends. Miss Golden admitted this, but is disappointed by the lack of promotion arranged for her work. It is a pity that Mr Abbeville failed in this respect, because this book will appeal not only to readers who can remember Miss Harlow, but to everyone fascinated by Holly-wood's happy years.

Miss Golden's main objective in compiling this book is to undo the harm done to the actress's reputation by a certain Mr Shulman who, some years ago, wrote a scandalous biography describing scenes in Miss Harlow's second marriage, to Mr Bern, accusing him of being an impotent sadist and dwelling on events of which only the participants could possibly have had any knowledge. Miss Golden's research contradicts all these sordid details, and she has even found pictures of Miss Harlow that make her look happy, healthy and natural, in contrast with the image of her looking like the head girl in a reform school, which most of us recall.

Last Friday, I was summoned by *House & Garden* to the home of a self-confessed interior decorator called Mr Osborne. This is the second time that I, who have never owned either a house or garden and who am known to be indifferent to what anything looks like, have been invited, if not to explain or evaluate, at least to describe the living quarters of someone whose tastes in the matter of décor are sufficiently refined to be of interest to the cognoscenti. Last time this occurred, my assignment was the apartment of Mr Michael O'Donoghue, who used to rule *Saturday Night Live* and who was kind enough to allow the movie crew of *Resident Alien* to invade his home. As I had met him socially, I was less intimidated by the task than by the present confrontation. However, Mr Osborne turned out to be most gracious – even cosy.

I have received a bizarre letter from a gentleman living in Cedar Grove. (Though this town has such a romantic, Mediterranean name, it is in fact in the middle of New Jersey.) He tells me that he is compiling a list of quotations on the subject of success from people who, in his opinion, have achieved this blissful state. Inevitably, this being America, most of the names mentioned are from the world of entertainment, but Mr Joe DiMaggio, Mr Arthur Ashe, and several politicians are included. Many of the sentiments expressed are slightly sanctimonious and some go so far as to mention You-Know-Who, although we all know how wholeheartedly He despises anything remotely like earthly happiness.

I have seen *The Player*, directed by Mr Altman from a book written by a Mr Tolkin and adapted by him for the screen. It is a relentless satire of the movie industry.

I like movies about movies. Usually they provide actresses with the opportunity to play actresses, which they do with special relish. This newest picture on the subject is different. There is a huge party at which we glimpse various celebrities playing themselves, but Mr Tolkin's main theme is the utter ruthlessness of executives in their dealings with frantically tenacious authors. The hero, if such he can be termed, is played by Mr Tim Robbins, who becomes increasingly desperate as his power is threatened by an even younger man played by a Mr Gallagher. At the same time that he is trying to cope with this situation, he is constantly receiving insulting postcards from a disgruntled author. Thinking that he knows who the sender is, he finds out from the man's girlfriend where he is, meets him, and murders him. At his victim's funeral, he meets this young woman who confesses that she doesn't really feel the required grief. It transpires that she is worse than a man – nay, worse than a studio executive: she has appetites but no emotion. At the end of the film, she marries Mr Robbins and they live ruthlessly ever after. The girl is played by Miss Scacchi, whose heartless indiscretions caused Mr Ackland to kill himself in *White Mischief*.

Throughout *The Player*, writers are for ever trying to interest Mr Robbins in their scenarios. They visit his office, they waylay him in corridors, they walk backwards in front of him, gibbering, as he goes to his car. One of these men tells him the tragic story of an innocent girl who is wrongly sent to the gas chamber. When we watch a preview of this film, it has acquired a ludicrously happy ending. This sequence is one of Mr Altman's funniest effects, but it is naughty. In *I Want To Live*, Hollywood *did* send the guiltless Miss Hayward to the gas chamber, and the incident contained one of the most telling lines in the history of film-making. As the prison warden straps Miss Hayward into the chair, he says, 'When you hear the capsules fall on the floor, take a deep breath.' He is trying to help her to make her agony shorter. In *The Player*, finally one of these innumerable screen writers tells the executive over his car telephone the story we have been watching. Mr Robbins likes it. Thus ends one of the neatest, most entertaining, most cynical films I have ever seen.

The very moment that Miss Dietrich's heart stopped beating, my telephone started ringing. It was almost as though she had been a member of my family. In fact, I never even met her, but in her heyday she certainly occupied almost all my thoughts. I adored her obsession with her screen image, but this opinion was not universally shared. When I saw *Morocco*, a girl sitting behind me muttered, 'She ain't 'alf stuck on 'erself.' In the 1930s, in the sad

London cafés where the more outrageous and the more helpless 'gay' boys congregated, a perpetual war of words was waged. Which was the more beautiful – Miss Garbo or Miss Dietrich? Really there was no way of comparing the two. The English press was for ever printing photographs of Miss Dietrich with captions such as 'The shadow across Garbo's path', but the two stars occupied different firmaments. Miss Garbo represented a remote, poetic yearning, while Miss Dietrich personified a worldly indifference.

Miss Garbo, though almost reverentially admired in Hollywood, was not popular there. Miss Davis said that this was because she invested most of her money outside the United States. Miss Dietrich, on the other hand, while claiming that she never liked making movies, loved America, and enriched her patriotic image by going to Europe to entertain the troops, often in situations fraught with danger. Hedda Hopper, who hardly ever praised anybody, said of her, 'That woman can do no wrong.'

I have been given a copy of *Marlene*, Miss Dietrich's autobiography. It is a fascinating book presenting a person very different from her screen image. In real life, she was highly emotional, but cynical; very feminine, but by no means frail; hard-working, but resentful of exploitation. Mr Siman, who wrote *Pizza Face*, a study in physical hideousness, has now turned his attention to the subject of beauty. He took me to lunch at Jerry's on Second Avenue to question me about my thoughts on this topic. To my surprise, he had been told by someone else whom he had interrogated that the most beautiful is that which arouses the greatest sexual excitement. I formed my ideas on beauty from movie heroines, and none of the women I admired had anything to do with sex. (If snowbound for a night in a wooden shed with Miss Garbo, all the men I have ever known would have been terrified.) What she and Miss Dietrich and Miss Del Rio radiated, at least from the screen, was a slightly sorrowful nobility, and that, to me, is an essential ingredient of beauty.

*   *   *

On Wednesday, I was invited by Mr Cook, who used to rule the Actor's Playhouse, but who now reigns over the Cherry Lane Theater on Commerce Street, to see a play called *Hauptmann* by a Mr Logan. I was privileged to sit next to Miss Kim Hunter, whom I have admired ever since I saw her co-starred with Mr Niven in a movie entitled *A Matter of Life and Death*.

Hauptmann I found interesting, but it worried me. Firstly, I thought its title a mistake. While no one will ever forget the name of Mr Lindbergh, I doubt that many people now living recall that the man who may not have kidnapped his baby was a Mr Hauptmann. Once it dawned on me that the play was about this famous court case, I couldn't help wanting to know if the accused was guilty or innocent. In a programme note, the playwright says that it is not the purpose of his play to refute the prosecution's case. This left me wondering what exactly its aim is.

After the show, there was a first-night party in a neighbouring bar which, for a few hours, became a mini-Sardi's with all the customers applauding the entrance of the star. While there, I was able to discuss the play with Mr Cook. He has always disapproved of the Lindberghs on the grounds that they were fascists. I felt that their attitude and that of other aristocrats such as the Duke and Duchess of Windsor was less a political stance than a hideous social snobbery – that all they wanted was for the world to be ruled by gentlemen. Mr Cook's dislike of the Lindberghs led him to suggest that it was they themselves who had murdered their baby. What a play that idea would have made!

On Monday evening, with Mr Cook and his constant companion, I was invited to an evening meal in the home of Miss Hunter and her husband. They live near the Cherry Lane Theater. Among the guests were a Mr Zindel and his wife. I didn't know until later that it was he who wrote *The Effect of Gamma Rays on Man-in-the-Moon Marigolds*, and that he is a Pulitzer Prize winner. Never before have I luxuriated in such a cosy, and, at the same time, rarefied atmosphere. Mr Cook questioned Miss Hunter closely about the experience of playing Stella in *A Streetcar*

Named Desire. She told us some fascinating things – among them that, during a scene with Miss Leigh, there were so many takes that, after a while, she rushed over to the director to ask him what was wrong. He replied that he was hypnotized by seeing that tears came into Miss Leigh's eyes at exactly the same moment of each take. It was a truly fascinating evening.

Summer

I am becoming more American

In my neighbourhood, traffic was in chaos this week because some kind of street fair was in full swing. Someone explained that the same objects are offered for sale at all New York's open-air markets. The vendors simply pretend that they and their wares are Italian one week, Ukrainian the next, and so on all summer long. I found this information hilarious.

The week has been shrouded in failure. On Thursday evening, I had been asked by a Mr Gordon, whom I do not know, to go to the Astor Place Bookshop and to read to its clientèle. It was fortunate that I telephoned before setting out for this illustrious emporium because I was informed by a member of its staff that Mr Gordon no longer worked there, and when I asked if, in that case, my presence was not required, the young lady said, 'I guess so.' She seemed slightly amused and offered no apology. I was surprised: I regarded this somewhat offhand method of dealing with what was, after all, a mild betrayal, as almost un-American activity.

The next night, I was supposed to hear one of the remaining Beatles perform at Radio City Music Hall. I reconstructed myself elaborately and sat, with one ear cocked towards the telephone, like the dog on the famous 'His Master's Voice' gramophone record label, but silence reigned throughout the evening. It has since transpired that I was given the wrong date by my proposed escort's brother.

I was therefore broken and disillusioned as I set out for Providence, Rhode Island on Sunday morning. However, the train journey cheered me up. I like travelling by rail: it is a situation in which no one can blame you for doing absolutely nothing but looking out of the window for several hours. Rhode Island is mostly water, but what landscape there is is picturesque, and Providence is quaintly Puritanical. The houses are made of wood, except for a few beautiful pseudo-classical public buildings such as the courthouse, in which I imagine that, with any luck, you might be condemned as a witch.

At the station, I was met by a fully representative group of three people – a white man, a black man, and a woman, the latter of whom explained that she had only been invited because it was her car we were using and her credit card with which everything was paid for. She appeared to accept her fate with surprising calm. As it was about half past three in the afternoon, we immediately went to a café for an all-purpose meal over which what was expected of me was explained.

The purpose of my visit to Rhode Island was to try to justify *Resident Alien*, which was being shown at the Avon Cinema, an 'art house' which the gay and lesbian folk of the city had taken over for several days of 'unusual' films. When, after signing a few books, we left the premises, people were lining up to see Mr Jarman's *Edward II*. The audience was extremely friendly and only asked benign questions, chiefly about my life rather than about the movie. I was on familiar ground and gave the usual answers in the usual way.

The following day, I arrived back in New York just in time to rush home and telephone a Mr Vincent, whose fair name was written in my sacred book in the space designated June 15. I had never met him and could not remember what on earth I had promised to do for him. The number he had given me was of a department in the United Nations building. I was terrified, but he turned out to be a very cosy gentleman who only wanted to take me to the elegant home of an elegant gentleman named Mr Kooder. The occasion was a party given for some of the members of a group called ILGA – International Lesbian and Gay Association. This is a formidable organization, but the party was extremely urbane: I don't think an outsider would have been able to guess anybody's guilty secret. However, they fully intend to change the world.

In the taxi on the way to the party, the conversation of my escort had already given me an inkling of the devastation likely to be caused by his iconoclasm and that of his friends. His view of what is usually meant by the words 'consenting adults' is a case in point. He thought that the age at which this hazardous status could be deemed lawful is thirteen. Another conventional notion that he challenged was the meaning of the phrase 'in private'. He wished it to include sequestered areas of public parks. Where, I asked myself silently, would it all end? Though I did not voice my misgivings to my kind companion or any of his friends, I could not help wondering if a worldwide gesture of defiance of the established order would not one day be regarded as based on what could be termed 'the Spartacus Fallacy'.

Yesterday evening I went to that frightening section of East 9th Street that is just beyond Revolution Square. My steps might have faltered in such a benighted neighbourhood had not a total stranger by some occult process divined what my destination was and led me almost to the very door. I was going to the home of a Miss Sharif who, from time to time, very generously transforms her living room into a mini-theatre. Some time ago, I saw a production there of *No Exit* by Mr Sartre.

The offering this time was *The Lover*, by Mr Pinter. It is about a married couple that tries to keep their sexual interest in one another alive by enacting various charades in which he pretends to be all sorts of different types of men whom she meets in bizarre circumstances, or he plays the husband jealous of these men. Though I am sure it was not intended by the playwright, this plot has relevance to the love lives of many homosexuals. In those far-off days when there was still a marked difference between the sexes, homosexual men frequently played at a heterosexual relationship with one partner parading a worldly competence that he did not really possess, and the other, an excruciating femininity which was sometimes a considerable handicap. Later, different masquerades emerged. Young men who had never seen a horse began to wear full Western gear; boys who couldn't even catch a fly – let alone hurt one – donned stormtroopers' uniforms. I have never understood how these disguises can hold up for more than ten minutes. When a pseudo-Westerner is asked by a prospective partner about his ranch, or a fake stormtrooper is questioned about his regiment, does not the entire subterfuge collapse? Moreover, what is the use of desire provoked by or admiration bestowed upon someone whom you are not? Even while watching *The Lover*, I couldn't help wondering when the married couple would stop pretending and collapse in totally asexual laughter.

On Sunday afternoon I was taken to East Hampton. It was a long journey – so long, indeed, that halfway through it we had to change cars like the coachmen of Wells-Fargo changing horses. At about five o'clock, we arrived at a clearing in the jungle ominously called The Swamp, but which turned out to be two picturesque barns with an open-air space between them occupied by garden furniture and one sumptuously upholstered chair that someone must have transported from her home specially for me. On this I sat for some hours and, though the sky was cloudy from one horizon to the other, no rain fell.

The occasion was a gathering of members of Thursday's Child, a benevolent organization devoted to the care of people with AIDS. Raffle tickets and T-shirts were for sale and there was an abundance of food and liquor to consume. I sat beside the ticket seller, ate and drank everything that I could lay my hands on, and talked with anyone who approached within a mile of me until about seven o'clock. Then my throne was carried into one of the buildings which transpired to be a pitch-dark twitching area where a Miss Rapp sang with great gusto some highly subversive political songs and a Mr Cohen read a passage from one of my books. Thereafter

I answered questions from the audience until it was about nine o'clock and time for me to go home.

The task of driving me back to Manhattan was nobly undertaken by a second Mr Cohen, the older, bigger, bolder brother of the first. I had been offered the opportunity to stay overnight in East Hampton, but had declined it because it is now very difficult for me to sleep a night away from my room. Because of my eczema, large areas of my wretched body have to be swathed in bandages to prevent me from clawing myself until the blood gushes out of my wounds and down the stairs with a gurgling sound. This, naturally, I did not mention to my escort. He did not complain, but my feeling of guilt was great and increased as time crawled by and progress became slower and slower. Everybody in America seemed to be converging on New York.

In prehistoric times – that is to say before I began to write this diary – I was once transported by car to Danbury in the middle of Connecticut. There, a movie, which it would be polite to call experimental, was being made. The scene in which I took part happened in a disused shop that, for the film, had been disguised as the canteen of a mental hospital. The only piece of action that I can now remember occurred when two handsome young men in white coats appeared and dragged the star of the picture out of the room. Now, many long, dark years later, a soundtrack that will narrate the entire story is being prepared, and what a wild tale it is!

I gather that several versions of this saga have already been attempted. The one in which I was involved was recorded in an upper room in that part of New York University that is situated on Broadway and Waverly Place, and that, from the outside, looks like a very modern cathedral and, from within, like a newly-erected shrine to the gods of DIY carpentry. My reading was supervised by two (presumably) superannuated students who, considering my various inadequacies, were positively indulgent and who took me to supper in a nearby café when the ordeal was over. The contempt felt by the young for the old which so disfigures English society seems to be totally absent from life in America.

One mystery arising from this assignment remains unsolved. Why did the makers of this film ask me to record its soundtrack? When, in a play about Mr Wilde by Professor Bentley, I played the part of the elderly Lord Alfred Douglas, critics described me as sounding like 'a nasal Mr Magoo'. It was not a kind description, but it is funny and undeniably accurate.

As though this new profession of being a 'voice-over' were not bizarre enough, I have now entered another unexplored kingdom: the comics.

In that restaurant on the corner of Second Avenue and East Fifth Street that has become my dining room, I met Mr Russo and Mr Wong who, between them, produce a comic magazine called *Jizz*. They presented me with a copy of its ninth issue. In captioned pictures, sometimes at the rate of twenty to a page, this tells the story of an attempt by an enemy of Mr Russo to incriminate him in a plot to kill the President by sending to the White House a letter signed with Mr Russo's name. Some of the wording is hilarious – e.g., 'questioning my parents about me is like asking a blind man about colour.'

Even more amazingly than the contents of this magazine was its cover. There, printed in full colour on glossy paper, was a picture of a gathering of people warming themselves at a fire in a dustbin, and most conspicuous among them was me. Does this mean that, after seeking recognition so vigorously and so unsuccessfully from so many sources, I am at last to take my place beside Mr Mouse and Mr Abner?

While we ate, Mr Wong, the magazine's illustrator, drew from a vast canvas bag a large sketch book filled with 'life' drawings. I have never deliberately read 'the funnies'. But, by chance, I have caught sight of a strip cartoon called 'Big Ben Bolt', and I was quite amazed by the skill and accuracy of the drawings. Mr Wong's work is also astonishing: it is far from naturalistic like the old-fashioned cartoons, but not because of any lack either of observation or competence. It is distorted by a consistent and highly stylized vision. However, my admiration turned to stark terror when I realized that Mr Wong was showing me these drawings not merely to solicit my approval, but also in the hope that they would persuade me to pose for him. I hastily explained that the time for me to pose nude was long since past, and this sad fact he graciously accepted. It was decided that he should take pictures of me fully clothed and work from them. He wishes to make huge paintings of The Seven Deadly Sins, and he thinks that I would be the ideal personification of Pride. I did not protest: he was paying for my lunch.

I am becoming more American. This is a change that I have always earnestly desired, but I now realize, alas, that it is the more blameworthy characteristics of my adopted nation that I am acquiring. Everyone, including Americans themselves, is for ever accusing people in the United States of having short attention spans – a phrase that, until a few years ago, I had never heard, but which, to my shame, I am now aware applies to me.

In the course of a single evening spent watching it on television, I tired of the Democratic Convention. It seemed to me that the same vaguely optimistic, self-congratulatory sentiments were uttered over and over again – that I was hearing what Mr Macbeth would have called 'a tale told by a Democrat, full of sound and fury, signifying nothing.' Friends tell me that, on subsequent evenings, these notions were expressed with considerable eloquence, but by then I had turned my eyes and ears elsewhere.

The Japanese recovered from being literally flattened by devoting themselves body and soul to their employers, by working harder for longer hours for smaller wages. But Americans think the solution to their nation's bankruptcy lies in demanding more from their government and by striking when their requests are not met.

* * *

All male homosexuals are missionaries at heart, and are for ever implying, if not actually stating, that everyone is really gay and either does not know or does not admit it.

The English branch of this enclosed order is now pecking at the long-dead corpse of poor old D.H. Lawrence. As part of this process, a Mr Robinson, who rules a company laughingly called Wall-To-Wall Television, and two of his merry men recently arrived in America to conduct interviews on this subject. One of these confrontations was with me and it took place at the Player's Club on Gramercy Park. This is a hushed, dignified institution full of old-fashioned portraits of people famous in the world of entertainment. I couldn't help wondering if whoever allowed these premises to be used for our programme knew what we were discussing.

The new argument about his sexual orientation is based on the undeniable fact that Mr Lawrence lavished much more enthusiasm and many more words on describing the physical splendour of his male characters than on the beauty of his women. Except for a paragraph in a story called 'The Ladybird', I cannot call to mind a single passage in praise of the features of a girl, whereas, when he discovers the gamekeeper's arm in *The White Peacock* completely fills his sleeve, he is deeply impressed. Personally, I do not think that this proves that Mr Lawrence was homosexual.

As I see it, he longed for the locker-room set-up, that celebration of manliness from which he was for ever excluded by his frail physique and his illness. Many people who suffer from tuberculosis have voracious sexual appetites, but this was apparently not so in the case of D.H. Lawrence. Mrs Lawrence described her husband as almost impotent. Once you have seen that famous photograph of the two of them standing side by side – she so huge, so self-confident, he so thin, so haunted – you understand his entire literary output. He never got his wife to do a damned thing he wanted. His novels compensated for his failure. Halfway through each book, we come across the sentence, 'She trembled before his dark beauty.' As with so many writers of lurid fiction, his writings describe the unlived life. Nevertheless, for all his iconoclasms, his insistence on using the shortest words for the longest things, the exhibition of paintings, so pornographic that they were seized by the police, I think he would have been horrified if any of his dream heroes had ever tried to use him as the instrument of their sexual gratification.

Last weekend I went to Baltimore. Every time I undertake one of these journeys out of Manhattan, I think it will be the last gesture that I am obliged to make on behalf of *Resident Alien*. Then another excursion is proposed, and I stagger on. This one was not difficult because Mr Nossiter and his newest true-love, a charming French girl, came with me and guided my steps towards the right train and led me from it at the right station. There we were met by a Mr Udel, who looks like the movie actor Sam Jaffe, but without the frenzied stare. We all rushed immediately to a radio station for a lively interview with a Miss Semione, who more or less rules the cultural channel of Baltimore, after which I was taken to a very grand hotel called the Colonnade, while Mr Nossiter and his friend were distributed among the poor.

Dinner was served at the strange hour of half past five in a restaurant of great splendour, whose staff remained admirably calm although our party of more than a dozen guests rearranged the furniture several times before finally settling at a table of da Vincian length. There I sat next to Mr John Waters, who is king of Baltimore and makes all his films there, including *Pink Flamingos* and *Hairspray*. He and Mr Nossiter indulged in a disparaging dialogue concerning field distributors, which might have been positively venomous had not Mr Waters been aware that I might repeat everything he said.

Incidentally, he told me that, in a time so long ago that the television play of *The Naked Civil Servant* had not been made, he paid me a visit in my room in Chelsea. I'm ashamed to say that I have no memory whatsoever of our meeting.

*   *   *

Last Friday, I was taken to lunch at the Café des Artistes by two young women who had come from England to test the climate of fashion in the United States. For some unknown reason, they thought that I would be knowledgeable about this subject. I explained that I am impervious to fashion – indeed, to change of any sort. This they found difficult to believe until I explained that I have not only been dressing in the same way for the past fifty years, but am still wearing the actual garments that kind friends gave me all that time ago – that I have never bought clothing since I came to America. In spite of this shocking admission, my hostesses remained calm and even paid for my lunch.

Behind me, as we sat and talked, a great deal of movement was going on. Lights were being adjusted; cameras were being focused. The centre of all this activity was Mr Charles Kuralt, the tele-visionary. For the entire time that it took us to eat, drink and talk, he sat at a nearby table with a plate of food before him (which he never touched). Whether this photographic session was intended to advertise him or the restaurant, we were unable to ascertain, but, at least to some extent, this incident compensated my hostesses for my lack of useful information on the subject of American fashion.

A few evenings ago I went to John's Restaurant on East 12th Street, where I found Jack Eric Williams and a coach party of his friends. There we ate as much as possible to fortify ourselves for a visit to the ruined public school on First Avenue, called Performance Space 122, where Miss Penny Arcade is doing a revised version of her show called *Bitch! Dyke! Fag-Hag! Whore!* This event has been reviewed in the *New York Times* without mentioning its title, which was considered too wicked to name. We all had a good idea what we were in for but our most unnerving expectations were not merely fulfilled; they were surpassed. There were more dancers, more nearly naked, twitching more violently to louder music than ever before. It was like *Hair* but angry instead of jubilant. Miss Arcade hates everything except sex. Her rage extends as far as the critics because they do not mention the names of her dancers.

At one moment, everyone, including some members of the audience, was jumping up and down. It was, as someone remarked, a 'very Sixties' event. I am happy to say that the dancers had been warned not to try to involve me. Even so, I was frightened. For me the show was saved by some wonderful lines such as 'Lesbians don't like you if you're a straight woman – unless you're battered' and 'If you're bisexual, lesbians think it's because you're not trying hard enough.'

Mr Jon Winokur is a complier of books rather than a writer of them. In modern times, he is a recycler of phrases. In the past he has been kind enough to send me *Writers on Writing*, *The Portable Curmudgeon*, an anthology of unkind remarks about the world, and *The Curmudgeon's Garden of Love*, a collection of cynical observations on human relationships. Now I have received *True Confessions*, a goldmine of revelations about famous people by themselves.

In this latest book, needless to say, Miss Madonna is the richest source of self-revelation: pages are devoted to her utterances while only paragraphs or single sentences are contributed by others. Among other confessions, she says she is not really a sex maniac – that she would rather read a book. Perhaps she is thinking of her bank book.

Many of the quotations are very funny but few are really peculiar. Perhaps the oddest comes from Miss Kinski, who says she used to eat her eyebrows. (Should she have been called Nastassia Kinky?) To me the most interesting piece of gossip is divulged by Jackie Cooper. He says that, when he was seventeen, he had a brief affair with Miss Crawford, who at that time would have been in her early thirties.

On Thursday afternoon, I went to meet two young men who had come to New York to climb the Empire State Building and to see me. In England, they had been performing a stage version that they had written of *The Naked Civil Servant*. The day was so crowded with engagements that I had to ask them to accompany me to the Ziegfeld cinema to see *Death Becomes Her* with Jack Eric Williams and sundry friends. To my relief, my new acquaintances were well received by Mr Williams. To my horror, he asked them if they were lovers, but they took this intrusion upon their privacy calmly. What they thought of the movie, I have no idea. My own feelings about it were worse than mixed. Mr Williams has a genius not only for discovering restaurants where the food is uneatable but also for finding cinemas and dim cellars where the shows are unwatchable.

The story of *Death* is about an ageing actress (Miss Streep) who visits a sorceress who gives her a potion that will make her young again. Her arch-enemy (Miss Hawn) receives the same rejuvenating treatment. Then both women try to nag Miss Streep's husband (Mr Willis) into trying it. He refuses, wisely regarding eternal life as something no one would wish on his worst enemy. Miss Streep, as always, flings herself whole-heartedly into the part, sings a cabaret number and nearly dances. She does not have a natural flair for comedy but she is better than adequate. The special effects are nothing short of miraculous and the editing is superb, but the plot is so farcical that, about halfway through it, it becomes impossible to care what happens to anybody. As our party was almost the entire audience at the Ziegfeld, what the world will think of this film, I have no idea.

I have a friend who rules Bloomfield in New Jersey and who, from time to time, sends me nuggets of eternal wisdom. Recently, I have received from him a clipping out of a paper called *The Star-Ledger*, describing experiments conducted by two scientists working at the medical school of the University of Southern California in Los Angeles. The article states that they have found that the brains of homosexual men are structurally different from those of heterosexuals: an area called the 'anterior commissure' is larger. This news has prompted my friend, who is an unquenchable optimist, to prophesy that these findings will instantly change the world's opinion of homosexuality – indeed will cause it to realize that gayness is innate and not a matter of wilful perversity.

I doubt it.

Firstly, scientific experiments take years to be accepted even by the experts and centuries pass before any new knowledge seeps into the consciousness of the man in the street of small-town America. Secondly, the objection raised by Pauline Christians to the gay community is less to its nature than to its behaviour. Whatever our instincts may be, we are expected to control them. In any case, prejudice is like a cactus: it flourishes without any discernible source of nourishment. I have conveyed these depressing opinions to my friend but I doubt that they will dim his rosy vision of a universally tolerant future. Surprisingly, I have received no reaction to this scientific information from any other quarter.

Occasionally I receive invitations to events taking place at the Public Theater on Lafayette Street. I seldom accept them, fearing they will be cultural in nature, but recently I pulled myself together and went to a screening of *The Water Engine* by David Mamet. When I've watched movies before at Mr Papp's theatre, they have always been quiet, slightly off-beat affairs. This occasion turned out to be rather grand. When I arrived, I found a large audience already wandering like caged lions around the vast entrance hall where three photographers were taking pictures of almost everyone. And Miss Miles was there.

The film is good. It has a beautiful colour constancy though it seemed to me too dark, but that may have been the fault of the projection at that theatre. The story, set in Chicago in the 1930s, is of a humble factory worker who invents a machine that requires no other fuel than water. This he tries to patent but, from the very beginning, his efforts are frustrated by agents of Big Business who are secretly determined to destroy his invention. Clandestine meetings are held with large men in huge limousines parked in deserted places. Offers are made for the machine but its creator does not want an outright sale: he is aiming at a royalty. Slowly

the situation passes from the eerie to the grim. 'They' blackmail
the inventor by kidnapping his blind sister and, when he still does
not give in, they kill both of them. We did not see the victims die;
we were merely told that their bodies had been found. I accepted
this tactful finale and assume that when this film is released the
world, which is for ever complaining that television is too violent,
will rejoice.

When the picture was over, a reception was held for Mr
Schachter, the director, and, presumably, for Mr Mamet who, on
the Hitchcock principle, has a small part in the film but, as I have
no idea what he looks like, I cannot say if he was there. Miss Miles
and I sat together and gobbled up whole handfuls of *hors d'oeuvres*.

I have been to hear Peggy Lee in cabaret at the Hilton Hotel on
Sixth Avenue and 53rd Street. Never before have we been treated
with such deference. The manager of the cabaret came to our
table, soon after we arrived, to welcome us and, after the show,
introduced us to Miss Lee who sat in another part of the hotel to
receive her fans. She was wonderful. She hadn't the faintest idea
who I was but, after a flicker of bewilderment directed towards
the manager, she graciously pretended that she did. When I praised
her performance, she replied, 'It could have been better,' with just
that hint of self-mockery reminiscent of Mae West – whom, minus
the sexual undertone, she greatly resembles.

Her audience was mostly middle-aged couples who obviously
knew her and her repertoire well. Before she had uttered the first
words of such favourites as 'Fever' and 'Is That All There Is?'
they were already applauding. She was in complete and effortless
control of her audience, her material and the microphone (in spite
of the fact that, at one moment, it fell apart in her hand). She did
not sing one decibel louder than audibility required, but every
possible shade of meaning was expressed.

In a humbler setting I have met an unknown relative. I only ever
had one cousin whom, because he was fatherless, my mother said

that my brother and I must treat with special kindness. Needless to say, we instantly decided to give him hell. He survived this treatment, grew to manhood, married a woman I only met once and sired four daughters whose names I never knew. One of these girls married an American artist whom she met while, as is the custom in the US, he was waltzing round Europe at the taxpayer's expense. They settled in Baltimore, where they raised three children.

Suddenly, after half a century of silence, the son of this couple telephoned me to say that he and his girlfriend would like to see me. We met in my local diner, where I asked how he knew of my existence since I have changed my name, my country of residence and so much else. 'We've all known about you for years,' he said. 'You were the homosexual in the family.' On hearing these words I had one of those rare glimpses of myself as others see me. I had never before thought of myself as the family's dark secret, the black sheep, the skeleton in the cupboard. I recalled that television conversation between Mr Harvey Fierstein and an interviewer in which he growled, 'Well, Barbara, every family has one.'

On Wednesday evening I went to the Rainbow Room on Rockefeller Plaza to meet Jack Eric Williams, who had managed to secure us a table at *Say It with Music*, the Irving Berlin revue. The Rainbow Room, though very grand, is not an entirely satisfactory setting for a cabaret performance. It is wide rather than deep and therefore compels singers to divide their attention between diners to their right and left, and the stage is so small that, what with a grand piano, played by a fabulous gentleman called Fred Wells, a double bass and a set of drums, it leaves very little space for the four singers. They had decided to add a visual component to the show by dancing about and waving their arms, which I found a little embarrassing. Nevertheless, *Say It with Music* provided a very enjoyable evening and the baritone, a Mr Raines, has a truly powerful and beautiful voice.

I once read an article which said that some of Mr Berlin's songs had been written so long ago that youngsters thought they were traditional airs. I avoided that mistake but I didn't realize that most of his earliest work consisted of wistful lyrics about lost love – *What'll I Do?* and *Remember*. The bolder songs in 4/4 time – *This Is The Army, Mr Jones* and *You Can't Get a Man with a Gun* – came later.

Autumn

*

How different Hollywood is from New York!

These last few days should really have been a time of mourning for me. My eczema has now begun to attack my eyelids, in consequence of which I rub them so furiously that one morning I woke up to find that I had a black eye. I could not hide my head in shame until the discolouration had, if not disappeared, at least diminished, because hardly a day has gone by this week without my being invited to a meal of some sort by a stranger – an occasion never to be missed. I do not know if these windfalls are occurring because September is the month when visitors flock to New York from altered states or because news of my infinite availability has been spread across the length and breadth of the land. I accepted the challenge at first by wearing dark glasses, though I knew people would laugh me to scorn thinking I was trying to stage a Garbo, and later by painting out the bruise with a stick of Erase given me by Jack Eric Williams. It was worth it. All my unknown hosts had amusing tales to tell.

A Mr Barefoot recounted how, when he went to England to stay in a private house, his hostess met his plane, did not greet him, drove him home in utter silence and only when the front door was shut behind them, spoke. Then her first words were, 'You are a great disappointment to me: I had expected you to be an American Indian.' Let that be a lesson to all travellers thinking of going to Britain.

A young woman I met in the Thompson Square Restaurant told me an even more delectable anecdote. When I mentioned that I live on the same street as some Hell's Angels, it reminded her that she had a friend who once occupied the very next house to theirs. After her home was vandalized by burglars, she appealed to one of the Angels to board up a window for her until it could be repaired. This he did. She repaid his chivalry by baking him and his confederates a heap of cupcakes which she decorated in icing with skulls and crossbones. I hope they appreciated that this must have been the first instance ever of witty cuisine.

Some time ago, Miss Arcade asked me to return to the public speaking racket at the ruined school on the corner of First Avenue and Ninth Street which will one day be renamed The Penny Arcade Theater. When I declined on the ground that I have already said it all – and often – she offered to interview me. This meant that I would be relieved of the burden of having to decide what on earth to say. I would merely be required to answer questions asked by her and possibly from members of our audience, if any. On this condition I agreed to her request and a series of five Sunday afternoons has been set aside for these public conversations. The first of them occurred last Sunday.

Dressed all in white like a Pierrot but without the huge black buttons and the black skull cap, Miss Arcade arrived at about half past three to collect me from East Third Street and take me to our destination. There I found a cosy setting complete with mock fireplace, two armchairs, a table, a tea trolley and a tea service. The performance, if such it can be called, began almost imperceptibly. A small audience of about forty people had arrived and we started to talk to one another and to them. Very graciously it transpired that what Miss Arcade longs to unearth in the course of this series of two-hour sessions is some hitherto hidden aspect of my nature. She obviously doesn't believe that my one desire in life is to please the public. She thinks – nay, hopes – that underneath my sickeningly ingratiating image there is another angry self waiting to burst forth. I am infinitely willing to cooperate in this voyage of discovery but I fear there is no hidden treasure at the end of it. What little you see is all you are likely to get.

* * *

Just as religion is for evangelists, not for congregations, and education is for teachers, not for students, so politics are for politicians, not for voters. The people who enter these professions are those who cannot live within their income of admiration. Most men search, in their spare time, for a woman who can be relied upon never to let a day go by without saying, 'How clever you are', or 'You're going to win – in the end.' This woman they marry and if, after a while, she ceases to utter the essential adulatory phrase, they move on to somebody else. There are, however, some men for whom, from the very beginning, the praise of one person is not enough. They become actors or, if the stage seems too hazardous a profession, they take to education, evangelism or politics. Such a man is the hero of *Bob Roberts*.

Bob Roberts is another political picture, not quite as fascinating as *JFK* but it features Mr Robbins, whom we last saw in *The Player*, and here he is even better. He plays an extremely right-wing candidate for the Senate who will stop at nothing to secure his election. He even contrives to stage an attempted assassination of himself and plants the gun on a persistent agitator. It transpires that this poor man has a withered right hand and, since the weapon in question is found in his right-hand pocket, he cannot possibly be guilty of the crime. He is acquitted and therefore has to be silenced by more direct means.

The critics have described this movie as hilarious and I cannot deny that the surprisingly sparse audience at the Paramount did laugh, although uneasily. I found it grim. It is very well and completely realistically acted, especially by the ill-fated revolutionary and by Mr Robbins, who plays a guitar at least as expertly as Mr Clinton plays the saxophone, and sings a number of songs, some of which are first-rate.

Two evenings later, I was taken to the Cocteau Theater on the Bowery to see *Under Milk Wood* by Dylan Thomas. I once met this strange man in Chelsea during the Second World War. Even in those far-off days he was famous, but chiefly as a drinker rather than a thinker. He was a tiny creature looking like a permanently surprised cherub. The programme notes tell us that he described *Milk Wood* as 'an extravagant play about a day's life in a small town in never-never Wales' and that is exactly what it is. It has no plot: it only narrates, in highly idiosyncratic language, how various townsfolk – the postman who knows the contents of every letter he delivers, the local wicked woman, a man for ever plotting the murder of his wife and so on – wake up, spend their day and go back to bed. The poetic language took some digesting but we became acclimatized and enjoyed the evening enormously. Ultimately it is a sad play. I have been to Wales: it is a dreary country – even worse than England – and, throughout *Milk Wood*, the audience is made inescapably aware of the monotony and the limitation of these people's lives in those days. Now, doubtless, they all have television sets and fax their love letters to one another.

The other day I was invited by the *maître d'* of a posh hotel to his home on the Upper East Side where he lives in mini-splendour. I had been asked to bring with me a picture of myself. I took two – one in black and white and another in colour, which is a postcard made from a painting done of me by a student when I was an art school model in about 1943. The purpose of all this was so that my host could embroider a likeness of me in coloured silks. I was shown a portrait done in this way of somebody else and very impressive it was. The stitches are so small that the shading on the face passes by imperceptible stages from light to dark. At a distance it could be mistaken for a painting. In my youth, I often day-dreamed that one day I would be sculpted by somebody famous and become monumental in bronze. I never imagined I might become immortal in silk.

My sessions with Miss Arcade at the ruined school on East Ninth Street continue. To my amazement, every week the audience is larger and Miss Arcade becomes angrier – not with me so much as with the world in general and the people of Oregon in particular.

In that state, she tells us, it is a punishable offence knowingly to employ a homosexual person. I had no idea the tide had turned so drastically.

As with Mr Noah and his dove, when I did not return to Britain any more it became known there that I had reached dry land and that therefore it was safe for all the other malcontents of the lost ark of London to fly westward. Among those who made the hazardous journey was a painter whom I had known for a long time in the days when I was only English. Over there, he had often resorted to giving his pictures away; once he alighted in Malibu, his work began to sell like hot cakes – almost like hot Hockneys.

Last week, on learning that a friend he had made on the West Coast was coming to New York, he asked him to telephone me when he arrived and this the young man did, calling himself Mr Stallone. He is really someone quite different but he has a Mexican name too difficult for ordinary mortals to pronounce. However, he is travelling with Mrs Stallone, who really is the mother of the movie star. She was here to rule a stall at the Whole Life Expo, which occupied two entire floors of the New York Hilton.

Mrs Stallone is an absolutely splendid being, festooned with ropes of pearls the size of chicken's eggs. She looks like a fortune-teller and, in a way, she is. She traffics in horoscopes. Within a few seconds of our meeting, she had asked me on what day I was born. When I told her my birthday was Christmas Day, she exclaimed, 'Ah, a Capricorn.' When I enquired if that was a good thing, she pointed out that it was the birthday of Jesus of Nazareth but did not say if that meant that I could save the world. I then went with the new Mr Stallone to another part of the hotel where he very kindly bought me a drink and gave me news of my friend in Malibu.

The Whole Life Exhibition was unbelievable, full of every brand of hazy philosophy, all manner of systems for prognosticating the future and any number of bogus diets and cures. I passed several people being massaged in all sorts of peculiar ways and in public. I even sat for a few minutes with a glorious black gentleman who passed his hands backwards and forwards within a few inches of my body and told me the story of my life. I loved every minute of it.

On Tuesday of last week, at the request of a Miss Metzler, I set out for Los Angeles. Never before have I travelled in such splendid style. A purring limousine arrived on East Third Street and took me to Kennedy Airport. There I took the MGM flight on which I found myself seated next to Mr Niederlander, who told me that he owned two theatres in Los Angeles and three in London, one of which was the Aldwych, where, in a time gone by, I saw Mr Shakespeare's *Antony and Cleopatra*, featuring Miss Suzman.

On arriving on the other side of the continent, I was met by an even grander limousine and whisked away to the Mondrian Hotel on Sunset Boulevard. There it transpired that I was to work for a German advertising agency, one of whose clients manufactures West cigarettes. I am happy to say that no attempt was made to turn me into a Marlboro Man. Next day I was taken in a trailer, together with some dressers and two real photographic models, to a side street off Wilshire Boulevard. There, as I have come to realize is customary in America, two policemen were waiting to supervise the parking of our fleet of vehicles and to sit around during the proceedings. One of these handsome gentlemen wore a black eye patch and, according to Mr Goldammer, who ruled this wild venture, asked him to make a movie in which he could appear as a pirate.

How different Hollywood is from New York! When we were making *Resident Alien* (which, to my amazement, was being screened in Los Angeles while I was there), bystanders on the Lower East Side of Manhattan took a keen interest and many of them tried to get into the act. When I sat on a canvas chair in the middle of the pavement on Wilshire Boulevard, strangers hurried by with averted gaze.

After a while, we all crossed the street and, on the other side, I was photographed refusing a cigarette from a typically good-looking young man. Apparently the utter improbability of such an overture being made to me was the whole point of it all. Later, though I was no longer involved, another similar young man was pictured offering a cigarette to a mermaid. For this escapade, the entire crew went to the beach but I was allowed to return to the Mondrian. The homeward journey to New York was just as splendid as the voyage out but, on it, I did not sit beside a potentate. In fact, the seat next to mine was empty. Does this mean something?

I have also been to Chicago, where I had a simply wonderful time. The weather was like summer: in the streets people strolled about, staring into the sky and smiling seraphically. Mr Guy Ruggeri, who had arranged the entire trip, met me at the airport and took me to the Belmont Hotel, where I had stayed the last time I was with him. There a friendly atmosphere prevails and the staff is willing to 'do' my room with me still in it. I merely lifted my feet in the air while the carpet was vacuum-cleaned.

I did not work (if you can call it work) on the day of my arrival but, instead, was given an evening meal at Mr Ruggeri's home and shown a videotape of *The Boy Friend*, the stage version of which I had seen many years ago in London. The movie is much better. It recreates to perfection the look of a 1920s glossy magazine illustration. In those days, it was not possible to manufacture 'fast' dyes of really bright colours. Therefore fashion houses told women that to wear a bright red dress or a screaming blue coat would be vulgar. All furnishing fabrics and dress materials were in 'art' shades – phlegm green, old rose, ice blue – and these are the colours used in this film.

I started to perform at the Halsted Theater Center on Wednesday, did two shows on Saturday and finished on Sunday evening. I was supposed to explain the royal family of England and the politics of America. I have no knowledge of either subject but fortunately a local journalist had prophesied, in a very witty article, that I would digress from my theme.

I did. I explained that the folly of all politicians in this country is that they want to rule the world and be loved, and this is not possible. The problem facing America at this time is purely financial and it is useless to offer voters more policemen, more teachers or a comprehensive health service, all of which will further deplete our already meagre resources. Japan, which was flattened at the end of the Second World War, has now become the most powerful country in the world because every Japanese man of employable age agreed to devote his entire life to his employer, and work for longer hours for smaller wages. I suggested that, if the United States is once again to become the great creditor nation, its politicians must offer their constituents starvation. Mercifully, nobody hissed. From this kind reception, I do not conclude that anyone agreed with me. I already know that American audiences are the most indulgent in the world.

In recent times I have made the slight acquaintance of a gentleman called Mr Regan. He is of Irish descent but, unlike the rest of his unruly race, he adores the English. He used to rule a bar called The North Star where from time to time he staged events recalling wartime Britain. At one of these he managed to secure the presence of Millicent Martin. He now reigns over the Spotty Dog Bar and Unisphere Cocktail Lounge on Eleventh Avenue at 43rd Street, to which he invited me for a Halloween party. I endeavoured to decline because I try never to become involved in occasions of public jollification. It is a long time since I tricked and I have never treated but I did not offer these facts as excuses. Instead I told him that I couldn't put on funny clothes, to which he replied, 'But you're always wearing funny clothes.' So I went.

As a special inducement, he sent one of his helpers to collect me from East Third Street. This young man explained to our taxi driver that we were in no especial hurry. He said that, though he did not expect to live for ever, he would like to survive the next two hours. His words went unheeded. We careered through the streets, stopping, starting, swerving with alarming violence. However, we arrived at our destination with only our nerves shattered.

The Spotty Dog, completely renewed, was opened three weeks ago. It is now a spacious, well-lit restaurant, serving large portions of pleasant food. What kind of clientèle will habituate an establishment so far from civilization, I have no idea. On the evening I was there, very few of the customers were recognizable because of their masks and strange costumes. Even the waiter had, perched on his shoulders, a toy rat which squeaked when pressed in the right places. (Who would not?) Mr Regan wore white painter's overalls and a bowler hat. How he will appear on subsequent occasions I cannot say but he is always a very agreeable host.

Today an unknown gentleman telephoned me to tell me that he 'works out' for two hours a day at his local gymnasium because, if he did not, fat would begin to surround his pectoral muscles until he would need a brassière. He seemed to be apologizing for his habit of taking regular exercise but I don't know why he thought it necessary to excuse himself to me. I think everyone should spend hours daily in a gymnasium and I have often explained that a man cannot be considered handsome unless his neck is thicker than his head (think of Mr Tyson). The only reason why I have remained such a feeble specimen is that, when I was young enough for my shape to be capable of augmentation, I lived in England where bodies are never mentioned.

Last week I received an invitation from an unknown gentleman living on the Upper East Side of Manhattan. I took the Third Avenue bus up into the rarefied seventies and with some trepidation walked westward. The nearer I got to the park, the more daunting my journey became. Houses gave way to mansions. When I finally arrived at my destination, I found the door open because a man in overalls was tampering with the lock. A doctor appeared as I entered the marble hall but he retreated almost immediately, probably realizing that he couldn't cure me. I proceeded to an upper floor where I found my host living in slightly constricted splendour with a young man who absented himself from our meeting to cook vegetables for a delicious meal to which I was later invited because I had talked so much that night had fallen while my lips were still moving.

The conversation was chiefly about a movie called *The Queen*. This is a documentary about a drag contest that my host had organized in a time gone by. From 1959 to 1968, he had traversed the length and breadth of the United States and (himself in drag) presented this show. Only Dallas had refused to condone the spectacle of 'deviants' having a jolly time. The word 'deviant', which I would have taken calmly, caused him to fly into an ungovernable rage.

Now many long, dark years later, he wishes to re-release this movie and his dearest wish is that I should become some kind of spokesperson for the film. I will, but I felt it was only fair to explain that when, for the *New York Times*, I reviewed *Paris is Burning*, I incurred the undying hatred of the entire homosexual community, though I genuinely thought I was repeating what Miss Livingston, who made that excellent picture, had told me. This information did not daunt my host. He feels that my equable nature in the face of what he considers the false naïveté of interviewers equips me for this touchy assignment.

Unfortunately, the demon machine which was to have shown me *The Queen* had broken down so I cannot, at this moment, say what the film is like, but my guess is that it will be different from modern drag shows in that it will be less bizarre. In olden days men donned female attire in the hope (not always fulfilled) of looking attractive. I myself only put on a dress once in my entire life because I soon realized that it accentuated my maleness – what there was of it. In a suit and wearing a collar and tie, I looked effeminate – appallingly so – but in silk stockings my ankles looked like chicken's legs. Also, in a dress my collarbones were shockingly visible. Many of my friends seemed unaware of this adverse effect or perhaps they didn't care. They may have worn women's clothes for the feel of them rather than their effect on others. They felt beautiful so to hell with public opinion.

Nowadays, beauty is no longer the point. This sad fact was brought home to me last Saturday when I went to Limelight where a party was being given for Screaming Rachel. There, amid deafening music, the lurid lighting and the decorations that prevented anyone from having a clear view of anybody else, was a motley assortment of guests, nice young men casually dressed as though for an evening at home, real women scantily clad and a throng of beings from outer space, glittering with sequins and fluffy with ostrich plumes. They wore shoes with heels so high that they could no longer brace their knees and fishnet stockings through which whole haddocks could have escaped. Their faces were clown-white and their lips were the colour of uncooked liver. The wish to allure had given way to the desire to appal. Drag artists no longer wish to make us sigh: they want us to gasp.

Towards the end of my lifetime in England, I was introduced by a mad child psychologist to a married couple who lived outside London. After a while the psychologist faded from the picture but I continued to know the two schoolteachers. They seemed a cosy couple, exceptional only in their willingness to know me. When I left England, our association came to a quite natural end.

Suddenly, about a month ago, the wife telephoned me in great distress to tell me that her husband had announced that he was homosexual. I do not imagine that she expected advice; I think she wanted comfort. As they have no children, I asked, in a cautious tone of voice, if their marriage had been 'satisfactory' until now and she replied that it had. Two Sundays ago, she called again. The situation had become worse. Among her husband's possessions, she had found a videotape which she had watched and found 'disgusting'. Whether she had challenged him with her discovery she did not say, but he is obviously now in agony – either of guilt or of frustration. (He recently thrust his arm through a glass door and is now minus half a thumb.) The wife says they will separate. I replied, 'The sooner, the better.'

When I asked how, in an English suburb, her husband had made any homosexual contacts, she replied, 'Through his computer.' I was both amazed and appalled by this. I was aware that the once-so-antiseptic telephone had recently become tainted but if computers have given way to sex, then all is lost.

On Sunday afternoon, a transvestite came to East Third Street to escort me to a dim cellar beneath a Unitarian church in midtown where, on every second Sunday in the month, a gathering takes place of all the people of ambiguous gender in New York. There were men disguised as women; men disguised as men; women disguised as almost everything. What to me was so remarkable about this meeting was the total absence of bitchiness, of wrangling and of showing off. We celebrated my forthcoming birthday with a delicious cake and I was presented with a tiny lamp which, when rubbed, emits a faint, tinkling melody. I was delighted and humbled by the hospitality lavished upon me.

The following day I went to that part of New York University that is on Broadway at Waverly Place to try to re-do the soundtrack of a film that I have never seen. It has been made by some young men who may once have been students at NYU or may merely be pirates who hire the recording equipment available in that extraordinary seat of learning. However, by this time my voice had sunk to an unsteady croak and the whole assignment had to be cancelled.

I went home, had a good cry and, towards nightfall, was collected by an unknown man who had been dragooned by an unknown woman into taking me to her home in Brooklyn. Apart from Mr Cherry-Garrard's voyage to the South Pole, this was the worst journey in the world. Though we implored about eight of them, no taxi driver would take us on such a desperate trek. I couldn't blame them. Brooklyn is a terrible place and all who live there know they have entered an enclosed order. In desperation, we walked to the subway station at the corner of Broadway and Houston Street where we waited for a train that did not come for a long and dangerous time. When it did appear, we forced our way on to it and stood swaying perilously but unable to reach any fixture on which to hold. I have to report that this motley throng of strangers, though pressed into disgusting proximity, remained surprisingly calm – even cheerful. Arriving at our station, we still had a long, dark way to walk over pavements that have not been repaired in a hundred years. By a miracle, when we reached the right house, our hostess was just that minute arriving. Had we not been delayed by so many difficulties on our journey, we would have been compelled to stand in the bitter desolation of a Brooklyn street for some time.

It transpired that our hostess did not really know the gentleman she had obliged to collect me. She had imagined that he owned a car – a notion which he dismissed with a self-deprecating laugh. When he had delivered me, he went away, presumably to recover. The unknown woman and I entered her apartment and I drank tea while she tidied up the place and herself. She was obviously expecting a great throng of guests. Only one arrived. To him and me, she read her poems while my escort, who had by then returned, played a trumpet. This situation, in a muted way, was as bizarre as a James Purdy story, the strangest element being my presence. Why had I been invited? Did my hostess imagine I was a poet, a musician, a critic? For me it was, though harrowing, an enlightening experience but I'm sure that, as a guest, I was a complete failure.

A gentleman who lives in this house, on the same floor as I, used to put dead mice under the door of my room. Then the young lady who lived on the floor below me acquired a cat with the result that my tormentor ran out of ammunition. Now the woman and her pet have moved and the rodents have returned. This may mean that my journal will become even emptier than it habitually is. I may find myself living under 'mouse arrest'.

Winter

*

For that one mad day, I lived a charmed life

Another Christmas. Even as a child, I did not believe in Mr Claus. I used to humour my parents in the preservation of this embarrassing myth. 'How long,' I asked myself, 'are we going to keep up this charade?' However, that cynical posture has never caused me to denigrate other people's participation in the season's festivities nor has it ever prevented me from partaking of their Yuletide hospitality. Nevertheless, it is a slight relief when Christmas is over. I now return to the serious business of re-acclimatizing my much-abused stomach to its customary bed-sitting-room diet of baked beans on toast. I also begin the lonely task of replying to at least some of the kind cards and letters that I have received from friends and strangers during the past month.

This takes longer than you might expect. If you purchase a large number of overseas stamps, the post office clerk hands you a block of strange yellow stickers on which are printed the words, 'PAR AVION AIR MAIL'. Since these are a gift, I do not feel that I have the right to refuse them and, if I accept them, I must use them. It isn't easy. To protect the gum, each of these small labels is backed by a piece of white paper exactly the same size as the piece in front. It takes about five minutes, inexhaustible patience and long thumbnails to separate the two so that the front half can be affixed to an envelope. So far I am managing to reply to four letters a day.

Communications have arrived from near and far. One has come from Auckland in New Zealand. It tells me that over there girls are sexually molested at a rate of one in four and that one boy in ten meets the same fate. Almost all the letters from Britain congratulate me on having escaped and say that England is deteriorating daily with more and more homeless people lying on the pavements of the West End of London. Compounding this generally gloomy view, a parcel was recently brought to me by hand. It contained gifts and a long letter purporting to prove that AIDS is a genocidal plot against minorities being hatched by the government. As I am neither a doctor nor a pharmacist and, as I do not consider sociology a legitimate science or think that politics make the slightest difference to the lives of real people, I was powerless to endorse or disprove this notion; but it worried me until, reading further, I found that the writer suspected her telephone of being tapped and herself of being 'tailed' as she walked about the Lower East Side of Manhattan. These suspicions relieved me of taking her medical theory seriously. I offered to return the gifts but was told to keep them.

Of the parties that I attended the most enjoyable was a birthday celebration for the long-time companion of a photographer who once made a videotape of a conversation between me and Lord Montagu. In a time outworn, his lordship was mixed up in one of those scandals that the English public likes best. It concerned a gentleman of high degree. Though the English have a fatuous reverence for their aristocracy, they also envy it and secretly wish to see it brought low. Furthermore, this case involved kinkiness. Lord Montagu had given a party at which some young airmen had danced with one another. Oh fie! (This event took place in an era when a man held his partner instead of merely twitching in front of her.) The newspapers nearly turned pink with shocked excitement. The photographer says that the videotape of my talk with his lordship can never be shown even to a limited public while either of us is still alive because it contains some 'heavy stuff'. I have no recollection of anything that we said but I accept my host's judgement.

More recently I have attended a party that lasted more or less all day. On this occasion my hosts were a gentleman who went to Kansas City to teach what used to be called elocution and his sister who works for a record company in Los Angeles where she deals with what her visiting card terms 'artist relations'.

They are both dauntless. They had hired a purring limousine – complete with cordless telephone – to transport them from Virginia to New York where they collected me from my humble abode and took me to lunch at the Jockey Club, though none of us has ever so much as seen a horse other than the poor old nags that stand in the rain on the south side of Central Park. There I expected to be asked to leave but, instead, we were given a delicious lunch over which my friend's sister and I tarried while he visited a publisher on whom he hoped to foist a book telling drama students how to make a loud noise for a long time without becoming vocally tired. Of this project I wholeheartedly approved. I have never believed that people can be taught to act, but they can be told how to declaim and, in happier times before anyone was ever 'wired for sound', that was what they had to do. Nowadays, when actresses do not wear hidden micro-phones, they tend to scream, which simply will not do.

When we did not dare to linger in the Jockey Club any longer, we walked to the Plaza, of which I was slightly less frightened because I had been there on two previous occasions without mis-hap. There we were not expected to queue with the ordinary mortals but instead were ushered to a special table where, though we had only just stopped eating lunch, we embarked upon a sump-tuous tea. I have always thought that supplying background music in public eating places is the saddest job in the world so we loudly applauded the tea room's resident violinist. This he noticed and came to our table to ask what selection we would like to hear. We suggested the songs from *The King and I*, the words of which were known to the drama teacher, who went so far as to sing them. Even this did not cause us to be evicted. For that one mad day, I lived a charmed life.

A few days ago I received an invitation to go to an address at the bitter end of 23rd Street. On the very morning of the chosen day, another message came explaining that the original venue had been closed by angry creditors. I was asked instead to go to 45 West 21st Street. This turned out to be a sort of annexe to Tramps and is a grim building showing no sign whatsoever of festivity, but I bravely pushed open the big black door and found myself in a lobby lit only by the light from a box office window no bigger than that opening in the door of a speakeasy through which customers used to murmur, 'Al sent me.' To one side of the box office, a tinsel curtain thinly veiled a long room furnished with a bar and a lot of small tables. At the far end was a small stage on which, on this occasion, stood two more little tables. I was reminded of SNAFU, a dubious cabaret setting where I worked in a time gone by. The bar is situated so that only the person nearest to the stage can see anything; his fellow drinkers could only see him.

The event that I had been summoned to watch was a play being presented by The Two Per Cent Solution called *Jungle Winter*. There were no programmes, but a leaflet explained that this is a modern adaptation of *The Seagull* by Dr Chekhov. It is set in what might be East Hampton in the off-season but that is not the only surprise. Some of the characters are black and a woman who is hopelessly in love with the young playwright has turned into a man – an innovation that the rest of the cast and the audience seemed to accept with unusual calm.

I saw *The Seagull* in England so long ago that Miss Ashcroft, last seen as the elderly English lady in *A Passage to India*, played the ingénue, as aspiring actress seduced and abandoned by a successful writer much older than she. Dr Chekhov was a country physician whose view of his middle-class provincial clientèle was cynical to say the least. He thought that their idleness was what caused them to take their broken hearts so seriously. However, English audiences regard all his plays as tragedies. Even a woman justifying the perpetual wearing of black with the words 'I am in mourning for my life' does not raise a laugh.

*   *   *

On Friday morning at half past six, a total stranger telephoned me for a chat. On hearing my slightly drowsy response, he said that he had not looked at his watch and therefore did not realize it was so early. I would have thought the fact the world was still in utter darkness might have warned him. At half past seven someone telephoned me from England to ask me the difference between right and wrong (I am not making this up). I quoted the hero of one of Mr Munro's stories who admits that he has forgotten the difference between good and evil but excuses this lapse by adding that his mother also taught him three ways of cooking lobster and that 'you can't remember everything'. My friend seemed content with this anecdote and rang off. At half past eight someone called me from Australia. Realizing that it would be foolish to hope for any more sleep, I got up – which was sad because my only appointment was not until nightfall.

Many weeks ago I went to a recording studio to speak some lines from *Romeo and Juliet* for a movie of that name. Now the hour has arrived when this film, which is acted entirely by Mr John Hurt and a bunch of cats, has been shown at the New School on Twelfth Street to the students of Professor Brown. Whether this picture will ever be shown to real people in a real cinema I have no idea, but a lot of publicity is being accumulated, presumably in the hope that it will. I have become involved in all this activity to a surprising extent in view of the fact that my voice is used for the smallest number of lines. I assume that this is because I conveniently live in Manhattan and adore publicity – even other people's.

The furore began last Tuesday when I was taken to a television station on Eighth Avenue at 34th Street. I have only seen a fragment of *Romeo and Juliet* on somebody else's television set and had to confess that I didn't understand it in the sense that I could not imagine for whom it was made. The young lady who was interviewing me smiled uneasily because I was not trying to 'sell' her the movie. I too was slightly embarrassed.

Last Tuesday I went to the New School to be interrogated by Professor Brown. The evening, which was almost like a vaudeville show but which I suppose should be called a class, began with the professor asking the students what they had thought of *Romeo and Juliet*. One girl was even allowed to read a short poem which ended with the words, 'I go to the movies to escape my pets.' Another student scored a big laugh by saying that the film was miscast. In general it seemed that the picture had not been well received. The professor did not chide the class for its negative reaction. In fact, he explained that the purpose of his tuition was by no means to force the students to like whatever they were shown. I have never dared to ask what it is he is actually teaching.

Yesterday, in one last effort to promote *Romeo and Juliet*, I was taken to the Whitney Museum. I had been there once before to attend the Absolut Vodka party given for Keith Haring by Mr Warhol. On this more recent occasion, the long trestle tables had been replaced by small round ones among which what I should now call a guest wrangler walked with me until we found someone who knew me and with whom I could sit and drink champagne. Later, we were shown about half an hour of the movie whose total running time is more than two hours. I am happy to report that the interest of the audience was aroused. A moment comes in the film when a cat, which has forced its way into a cage and snatched up a bird in its mouth, is compelled to release its victim on being hit by a car. On seeing the bird fly away, everyone cheered. On realizing the cat was dead, everyone groaned.

This week my agent said I must go to Philadelphia in spite of all the terrible things W.C. Fields said about that entirely inoffensive city. She explained that I was to receive more than is usually paid to extras in movies, so I went. I believe that it was Miss Cher who said that being in a film was like being asked to swallow broken glass and I endorse that impression. Everybody was extremely kind to me, finding a chair for me to sit on during breaks, but the experience was absolute hell.

I was made to do the 'Madison', of which I had never even heard.
It turned out to be one of those old-fashioned dances involving
an *enchaînement* of complicated steps which have to be learned.
Actually, I stood in the background and moved minimally to and
fro because I am now too old to learn anything. Mr Drake, who
was once kissed by Larry Kramer and who wore solid gold boots
and a false moustache but very little else, managed to learn the
steps with astonishing ease: he even executed them as though he
were enjoying the exercise, but then, as we all already know, he
is an accomplished actor.

All the extras were appearing as guests at a conspicuously sinful
fancy dress party. A member of the crew asked a woman disguised
as a cowgirl if she was looking to lasso a cowboy, to which she
replied, 'Not at *this* party.' Among those present were a bishop,
a Monsignor, the Mona Lisa, a circus ringmaster and sundry other
ingenious masqueraders. This scene was photographed at night in
the apartment of two of the guests who surveyed the situation
benignly, though it is certain the place will never be the same
again when the movie colony has departed. To this vortex of
kinkiness Mr Tom Hanks, dressed as a naval officer, invited Mr
Denzil Washington, who will spend most of the film defending
Mr Hanks in a discrimination suit against a firm that has termin-
ated his employment because he has AIDS. The picture will be
called *Philadelphia* and is being directed by Mr Jonathan Demme,
a charming man who visited all his cast in their trailers to thank
them for appearing in his movie.

I think we began work at about seven in the evening, though
it is hard to guess the time because there is so much waiting to
be done. We were allowed an hour for 'lunch' at midnight and
crept home at four in the morning. Strange to relate, it is not
really cold in the middle of the night in the middle of January in
Philadelphia, though there are other hazards. One young man was
mugged on his way to the set.

A large room had been booked for me at the Omni Hotel, which
is not quite so vast as the Omni in Atlanta but is very grand. I

tried not to show that I felt out of place. When we all foregathered in the lobby, it transpired that a Mr Nyswaner, who wrote the script for *Philadelphia*, and a Mr Stoddard were also guests of the hotel. The latter gentleman was on his way to North Carolina to explain to the inhabitants of that state the new laws acknowledging the rights of gay couples. I forbore to explain to him that *The Last of the Mohicans* was made there and that he might be attacked by savages wielding hatchets.

On Saturday morning I returned to New York in a train crammed with passengers: evidently people leave Philadelphia more often than they visit it. In the evening of that day, I attended a party celebrating the thirtieth year of a partnership between two of my acquaintances. I was not alone with them for long enough to ask them how they felt about the new laws relating to 'significant others'. I sat next to a handsome escaped policeman who believes in acupuncture but, even so, this party seemed normal compared with the one in the film.

On Monday I returned to Philadelphia and reached the Omni Hotel just in time to fling my luggage into my room before being whisked away to the film set. This session proved to be less exacting than the previous one. I was allowed to sit down almost all the time – as a wallflower while others 'did the Madison' or as an amused spectator while entertainers performed. These were The Flirtations, a quintet of gentlemen who sang, 'Please, Mr Sandperson, bring me a dream' (decorum prevents me from describing what dream they had in mind) and Lipsynka, who was required to do her act four times. It never varied by so much as the twitch of a feather boa, which shows how highly professional she is.

I was released in time to snatch seven hours' sleep before returning to New York a second time. I now have a cold and am a nervous wreck but no one can accuse me of failing in my duties as a butterfly on the wheel. Despite my cold, I pulled myself together sufficiently to keep an appointment at my very own local diner with a Miss Goodkin, who works for *The Times* of London. She wanted chiefly to know about my childhood, a time now so distant that my memories of it may be only partly true, but I did my best. It is difficult to imagine readers of The Times being interested in me. That august paper has never enjoyed a reputation for sprightliness. One of Mr Coward's plays begins with a wife arriving at the breakfast table where her husband is engrossed in a morning paper. 'Anything exciting in the paper?' she asks brightly, to which he replies, 'Don't be silly. I'm reading The Times.'

On the evening of that day, I went to Mr Musto's birthday party, held this year at USA, a relatively new twitching area, situated on West 47th Street. Appropriately, the first person that I met when I arrived was the unquenchable Miss Miles. We proceeded to the bar where our host greeted us. His birthdays have become an annual excuse for a gathering of people in the 'fame game', at which he is an expert. He was wearing platform shoes, a suit made from some metallic fabric and a wild Afro hairdo. He seemed as tall as a tree – the one God did not make. Every time another guest arrived, more lights flashed. As someone remarked, there were more photographers present than victims.

After a while, we all proceeded upstairs to an eating area where Randy Allen appeared as Bette Davis. I did not think the performer was very well treated. For one thing, half her audience was behind her and, for another, the hideous music never ceased. But perhaps this jaundiced opinion was due to the fact that, by this time, I had begun to feel really ill. I'm ashamed to say that I left without saying goodbye to Mr Musto.

On Saturday morning I was interviewed by the BBC. If the interest in my childhood taken by The Times was not enough proof that the walls of British respectability have been breached, let this incident be added. The BBC used to be called 'Auntie' by those who worked there – a snide reference to its posture of perpetual avoidance of anything shocking. Moreover, it cannot be claimed that pressure is being brought to bear on it by the public. When a young friend was last in London, he was asked by a stranger if he had been in *Resident Alien*. He admitted that he had been, which evoked the comment, 'We're a bit tired of him over here but in America . . .' In spite of all this, I was summoned to 103 Second Avenue at eleven in the morning where a handsome Welshman questioned me about glamour. Why me? I said that glamour exists where all is present but not all is given. This seemed to please the organizer of the programme, so I repeated it several times and the interview passed pleasantly – especially since, at the end of it, I was paid in cash.

One morning at the beginning of last month, I stood for a moment at the open window of my room and, except for the very faint wail of a distant police car siren, there was no sound to be heard. I thought it was the snow that had hushed the usually strident city. Then I sat down and began to turn the pages of a newspaper in search of its crossword puzzle and it was as though I was handling some kind of flannelette. At last it dawned on me that I had become almost totally deaf. My agent, who also has hearing difficulties, says that I'm not missing much but I think she might be considered cynical. I liked the noise of Manhattan. It is said that we should beware of the ambitions of our youth because, in old age, we may achieve them. When I was young, at a time when my brothers wanted to be ships' captains or steam engine drivers, I only wished to be a chronic invalid. Now I am, but in a way that deprives me of the pleasure of long telephone conversations – especially with strangers.

In spite of this and other serious handicaps to communication, I went, at the invitation of a Miss Sherrer, to a branch of the School of Visual Arts on West 21st Street to speak to some students. They were gathered on the second floor, which has been partitioned into a honeycomb of small cells. Presiding over one of the slightly larger areas was a cosy professor who, to my amazement, had heard me when I spoke at the Players Theater on MacDougal Street some fourteen long years ago.

I tried to explain to the audience what an art school is like from a model's point of view – that the students have entered the college, not running eagerly towards art but creeping backwards, trying to avoid real life, and that they hate the model. When father asks his daughter what she intends to do when she leaves school, she thinks, 'Oh my God, it's a reasonable question,' and then, after a moment's panic, 'I know: I'll do art.' She then sits in the college canteen, necking, playing a guitar and smoking pot for four years, after which she becomes a typist. Though I detected no sign of consternation on the faces of my audience, fearing that this picture might seem unduly gloomy, I explained that these years need not be wasted, that they can become a time during which a young person decides who he or she is and how to process, package and market an image. It was hard to tell whether this message was understood, believed or even heard. There was certainly no outcry.

My contact with current events now comes less from actual experience than from reading letters and newspaper clippings sent to me by kind friends. Of these the most elating took the form of a letter from my spy for Key West. He tells me that many long dark years ago the Royal Academy of Dramatic Art staged a version of *Orlando*. At a small cocktail party after the show, the young Australian student who had played the lead said to Lord Kinross, one of those queer peers who gave the British aristocracy such a bad name, that she had acted 'a peculiar role in which she kept changing her sex.' To this his lordship replied, 'Not peculiar at all. People like that are all over London.'

The most distressing news refers to Mrs Riva's biography of her mother, Marlene Dietrich. We all know that, while a child's parents are alive – especially if the son or daughter still lives at home – never a day passes without renewed vows of vengeance upon either the father, the mother or both, but when the offending parent is dead – when the worst is over – cannot calm be restored? Cannot the past be forgiven and public memories, though largely untrue, be allowed to linger on the air like a fading perfume?

Miss Dietrich was not really such an indestructible beauty as, say, Miss Del Rio, but she was presented to us by Mr Sternberg and by herself with such hushed reverence that we believed in her beauty absolutely. As Mr Beaton said, 'What does it matter if she is really beautiful? She *feels* beautiful enough to convince anybody.' Even Mr Hitchcock, who never forgave any woman for not being Grace Kelly, called Miss Dietrich 'the supreme screen being'.

I have now seen *Orlando*. It is, as I guessed, unabashed festival material and can never be shown to real people. It is a slow but very beautiful pageant with long, sustained close-ups of the exquisite Miss Swinton in costumes ranging from Elizabethan through Queen Anne and Victorian to the present day. For me the most exciting moment at the screening came at the end when the new Mrs Sting, who was in the audience, introduced herself to me.

1993

Spring

*

*In the rest of the world, fame is something that happens to
you but in the United States it is something you do*

I have been trying to understand how Miss MacLaine manages to
suppress all feelings of weariness when she so enthusiastically
embraces the idea of reincarnation. Imagine falling out of your
mother's womb with the words, 'Here again.'

On the first Sunday that the weather was like spring, I was taken
to Chinatown to be interviewed by an English television company.
When I arrived, they were on Elizabeth Street in a vast, extremely
busy restaurant owned by a Mr Fong. They explained that they
had chosen this noisy, difficult venue because of the décor which,
as in all Oriental eating houses, is in bright red and yellow. I
was not interviewed there but, after the customary interval spent
drinking coffee in a van, I was transported to another street and
questioned standing on a sidewalk thronged with Chinese shop-
pers. I have no idea whether the streets were so crowded because
this was a special day in the Chinese calendar or because it was
the first day in a long while that it had been pleasant to be out of
doors or because this district is always so populous. It was hell. I
was asked what was wrong with the world. I managed to refrain
from saying 'the people' and said 'the music'. I have no idea if I
said the words the interviewer wished to hear.

I am not a dedicated theatre-goer but, in my late teens, I thought
I was and went to see a lot of highbrow shows. That was nearly
seventy years ago. Since then I have noticed a lot of changes in

show business – not all of them for the better. In recent years there has been no play as great as Mr Shaw's *Saint Joan* or Mr O'Casey's *The Plough and the Stars*. There has been no actress with the panache of Edith Evans and no singer as good as Gracie Fields, though this has not mattered because all performers are now wired for sound.

However, two components of theatre are better. One of these is the dancing. When I was young, a chorus boy (almost a term of abuse in England) was only required to put his arm round a girl, which he did with little conviction, and to kick his height, with which demand he had no trouble at all. Now young men are turning unsupported somersaults in the background while the leading lady is singing centre-stage. The second aspect of modern theatre which has improved is the staging. In the Twenties, it was as well for a dramatist to arrange his plays to require only one set because it took so long to change the scenery. Now, in no time at all and without even lowering a curtain, miracles are wrought: back-projections glow and fade, lighting re-focuses on different areas of the stage, props slide effortlessly back and forth.

The *Washington Post* has sent me a copy of Mr Shipman's biography of Miss Garland. The subtitle of this work is 'The Secret Life of an American Legend'. I would not have thought she had a secret life. Her behaviour was so outlandish that almost everything she did became instant public knowledge, but in these pages a few strange facts are revealed. Her father, though he married and sired three children, was homosexual and so outrageous with it that schoolboys in Grand Rapids made jokes to his daughters about how to obtain a pass into his cinema.

Unlike so many show business biographies, this is not a work of deconstruction; praise and blame are handed out with an even hand. All the same, it becomes impossible to like Miss Garland. She seems to have possessed no humility. She was placed under contract to Metro-Goldwyn-Mayer by the time she was thirteen years old and was a movie star at sixteen but she never seems to have been grateful. She wanted not the wages that would meet her needs, but a salary which would prove that Mr Mayer valued her as highly as Miss Durbin was thought to be worth to her studio.

After reading the book it becomes clear that Miss Garland was not naturally suited to being in the movie industry. She could not cope with the long hours and was for ever affronted by the peremptory commands of her directors. She needed a live audience whom she could bamboozle into thinking of her as a helpless waif who must be given all the applause in the world to get her through a single number, when in fact she was as tough as old boots but not as comfortable. I once saw her at an extinct cinema in London. She was a dumpy little thing wearing a suburban party dress and singing in a rangy, brassy voice in constant danger of cracking, but the audience went wild. When the orchestra had played the first few introductory phrases of a song that begins, 'I'm gonna love you like nobody's loved you . . .' people sitting near me were already sobbing audibly.

On Tuesday evening I went to Mr Papp's theatre on Lafayette Street for a symposium on fame, moderated by Mr Clive James, an Australian masquerading as an English televisionary, who has written a book on the subject. His guests were Mrs Ivana Trump, who, as someone remarked, has proved that there is life after Donald; Miss Liz Smith, who made the distinction, not usually appreciated in America, between fame and notoriety; Mr Harold Evans, who rules Random House, which will publish Mr James' book; Miss Anna Wintour, who described the spread of fame from fashion models to their photographers and even to their hairdressers; Mr Norman Mailer, who told various stories against himself and finally Miss Fran Lebowitz. Naturally she was the most interesting speaker. She said the best kind of fame was a writer's: it secured its possessor a good table in a restaurant but didn't provoke anyone to interrupt him while he was eating.

Sitting in the audience, I whispered to the young lady next to me that no one had pointed out that, in the rest of the world, fame is something that happens to you whereas in the United States it is something to do – a career in itself. The next day, this remark was quoted in Miss Smith's column. Her spies are everywhere!

I've been to Los Angeles.

I was frightened because, the day before I was to embark upon my journey, no airline ticket had arrived. When I told my agent that it seemed unlikely that I would go, she flew into a panic so great that she uttered the words, 'Buy a ticket.' This I thought would be going too far. Money is for saving, not for spending. However, our difference of opinion never degenerated into an unbridgeable rift because, on the very morning when I was due to depart, a kind lady arrived in a purring limousine and escorted me to Mr Kennedy's airport. On the other side of the world, I stayed this time at the Bel Air Hotel, and the high spot of my visit came when in the lobby I met Miss DeMornay, who was the star of one of my favourite movies, *The Hand that Rocks the Cradle*.

While I was in Los Angeles, my trembling steps were guided by a Miss Korenbrot (whom members of the hotel staff, apparently unaware that publicists are with you always, sometimes called Mrs Crisp). With her help, I was interviewed by the *Los Angeles Times* and many more papers and radio shows. At the final party to which I was invited while there I realized that almost all the men in Hollywood are lawyers and to be with them is like visiting a zoo just before feeding time. There are few exchanges of ideas; almost all conversations are deals.

I was worn out, but it was fun. Los Angeles is New York lying down.

The actual purpose of my visit to California was to meet Mr Jay Leno and to be on his television programme. He was charming and, on being told that if you can live on peanuts and champagne you need never buy food again, he handed me a bowl of nuts and opened a bottle of champagne. My spies tell me that he seemed nervous, but I did not notice this. I had a wonderful time.

I have now seen *Jurassic Park*. I enjoyed this film. The special effects, which are now the main attraction in all modern films, were spectacular. At one moment, a prehistoric flightless bird is seen to jump from ground level onto a counter. But it all remains 'kid's stuff'. It typifies a disturbing trend. Within living memory, I have seen a musical about broken hearts of railway coaches, managed to avoid another musical in which the entire cast wears cat-suits, and lived through a play, regarded as serious, at the end of which two grown men play with a balloon. It is no good claiming that this descent into puerility is a pandering to American tastes, because many of these shows originated in England – once the home of jaded sophistication. Nursery entertainment is now a universal vogue.

Now that I am a blasé veteran of two first features, I watched all these epics to see how much the actors have suffered. In *Jurassic Park*, two children and one adult spend about a quarter of the film covered with mud and drenched with rain. I could imagine them enduring this state of humiliation for at least two weeks – in which, every morning, a make-up artist, holding in one hand a Polaroid photograph of yesterday's final take and with the other smearing their cringing faces with some kind of brown paste and squeezing a wet sponge over their heads before pointing them toward the set. However, you can dry your tears: they were thinking of the money, the beautiful money.

Summer

*The only way to avoid being photographed in Manhattan
is to keep moving*

I have been to Cleveland – again. The last time I was there, it snowed. On this occasion, the weather was sunny and pleasantly warm. I was met by a charming young woman who works for Landmark Theaters and who took me to a hotel where the woodwork is always wet because it is owned by a Mr Glidden, who invented house paint. I was interviewed by a Mr Dooley and, later, by a Ms Connors. It seems that all journalists in Cleveland are Irish.

In the evening *Orlando* was paraded before the amazed eyes of the local inhabitants while I was given a pleasant outdoor meal, after which I faced the audience and tried to justify my appearance in the film.

At dawn the following day, I went to a television station, where I said the usual things in the usual way. Then a handsome gentleman called Mr Harris took me to his office, which is situated in a strange building that I dimly remember from my previous visit to Cleveland; it is a huge arcade covered by a glass roof and lined with chic shops on two levels. I was deeply impressed.

I have also been to Toronto – again and again. My original invitation to that fair city was my first intimation that the world had gone mad. In those days, I was only English and was asked to go to Canada at once just for the day. The second visit lasted two or three weeks, during which I worked (if you can call it work) in the Toronto Workshop Theatre. On my third sojourn, I was accompanied by Mr Nossiter, who had directed *Resident Alien*, which was being shown to the crowned heads of the festival circuit (including Mr Jaglom wearing his funny hat). This time I was there at the invitation of Reliance Releasing, personified by two delightful young women who housed me in the Four Seasons Hotel in great luxury. There I was interviewed from ten in the morning until five in the afternoon. I know I have a bad reputation for saying the same things over and over again, but what else could I do? I had a wonderful time but, as always, the greatest pleasure of travel is that it makes you so glad to be home – however dreary that might be.

My slavery to Mr Sony continues. I have now been sent to Miami. Before I set out, I was in some bewilderment as to what I would find at the end of my journey. Recent television pictures of the enduring damage from last year's hurricane had shown me Florida as a few water-logged planks lying beside a deserted road. When I mentioned my apprehension to my agent, she said, 'Those were the remains of the homes of the poor. The rich *never* get blown away.' I thought this remark unduly cynical, but she was right. The rich live on an island clearly visible from the mainland and there not a leaf has fallen, not a tile is cracked, not a brick has been dislodged.

I stayed at the Century Hotel on Ocean Drive, which also had remained unharmed. The proprietor told me that, until recently, the entire district had been a den of thieves and murderers; now it is a line of Art Deco hotels. The weather was burning hot, but the room in which I slept was cool. I remained comfortable until I was dragged on to the beach where, amid wind and sand, though fully clothed, I was photographed holding a surfboard. Where such a picture could be used I cannot imagine. *Orlando* was not yet showing in any of the local cinemas, so I was not expected to address an audience. Instead, I merely answered questions put to me by a local journalist and returned to New York.

*   *   *

Since then, I have been to Dayton in Ohio. There, once again, I found that the weather had been restrained for my sake. The river was not in flood. This engagement was not engineered by Mr Sony. It was a private event set in motion by the kind friend who, some time ago, took me to see *I Hate Hamlet*. In Dayton, *Orlando* was being shown at an art house called the Neon Cinema, to whose denizens I tried to justify the film. I really like Dayton: its inhabitants are inexhaustibly friendly. If I were not still waiting for the opportunity to rule the world, I could live there. During my stay, I was taken by my hosts to see *The Fugitive*. It is an excellent film: the excitement never flags, but its plot is so complicated that none of us could decide why Mr Ford's wife had been murdered. Mr Ford starts out with a beard, but soon shaves it off in an effort to avoid being recognized by his pursuers. This is a pity, because he looked very attractive when he was fully woolly.

Finally, I have been to Staten Island. It is riddled with culture and with history, of which the Islanders are justly proud. The occasion of my visit was a picnic organized by a politically active lesbian group called Lambda, in front of whose banner I was photographed. This event was sufficiently civilized for me to be able to avoid sitting on the ground, but the music was as loud as if everyone had been heterosexual. The members of Lambda are pinning their expectations of a happy future on the re-election of Mr Dinkins. I regard this as a forlorn hope, but did not say so – at least, not loudly.

On home ground, I was taken some time ago to the Helen Hayes Theater to see *Shakespeare For My Father*. This is a one-woman show performed by Sir Michael Redgrave's younger daughter. It does not hint at any of the gossip about him that so intrigued the English – his illicit liaison with Dame Edith Evans, for instance. Instead, it concentrates on the relationship between Miss Lynn Redgrave and her father, which greatly resembles the relationship between Mr Lear and Miss Cordelia. It took her most of her life to gain his attention, to say nothing of his affection. This fact helps the show, because it allows her appropriately to quote *King Lear*.

The evening is fully cultural, but never boring. On the contrary, it is both touching and funny. Miss Redgrave offers hilarious impersonations of Maggie Smith and Sir Noel Coward. She couldn't quite manage the prolonged wail, like the whistle of a distant train, for which Miss Evans was so famous, but perhaps it is a little unchivalrous to mention that, as she had already spent two hours reciting fragments from a number of Mr Shakespeare's plays.

The only way to avoid being photographed in Manhattan is to keep moving. The fact that I've been photographed between each of the above-mentioned events would not be worth recording if it were not for the fact that one session was so extraordinary. A young man came to my home to conduct me to an upper room on East Seventh Street where he placed thin strips of sticky tape across my face (as though he were preparing to execute a hard-edge abstract). Then he painted almost my entire face black. When this coating was dry, he added a few dabs of white and the result was photographed by his friend.

That was the easy part. The difficult stage of the proceedings was trying to remove the paint. Though it was watercolour, it could only be removed with soap. I tried not to complain, though, obeying laws set down by Helena Rubinstein, I have not washed my face with soap in the past sixty years. To my surprise I do not seem subsequently to look any worse than usual.

Of course, I consider that beauty is a complete waste of time – principally because, without even knowing it, we still cringe in the shadow of classical ideals of beauty. The Greeks were mad about the human body – so much so that during its heyday Athens must have looked like an outfitter's window during a weavers' strike. But it was no help: not one of the great classical statues has the least physical individuality which would make it desirable or even interesting. I regard the human body neither as the image of You-Know-Who nor as the temple of Miss Aphrodite. I would describe it as a gravity-resisting mechanism of extreme vulnerability in constant danger of going wrong.

Autumn

*

I thought I was in a jolly film. I was wrong

I have received a book of drawings by Mr Cocteau called *The Passionate Penis*. I cannot refrain from expressing a faint regret at finding that this man, whose movies I loved for their all-pervading but delicate poetry, was just as obsessed with the idea of the economy-size you-know-what as all those tiresome homosexual men I met when I was young and only English.

My term of slavery is drawing peacefully to its close. I have been sent to Austin and Tampa, on each occasion to try to justify the movie *Resident Alien*. Both these fair cities I have visited before. The last time I was in Austin I stayed in the home of a gentleman whose name I have sadly now forgotten, but whose garden I remember well because it was mostly vertical, descending by steps cut in the cliff face to a landing stage at the edge of the Colorado River. Apparently, this river was once a trickling stream, but has now been broadened by a dam into an impressive waterway on which, from my hotel window, I could see oarsmen sculling to and fro, whether singly or in crews of four, and at dusk could watch swans gliding by. The hotel was a very grand establishment called The Four Seasons, and was where the Queen of England (the other one) stayed when she graced Texas with her presence. I spent most of my three days there sleeping or eating – including an open-air breakfast. Between meals, I was taken by car to survey the surrounding landscape: mostly parched grass and crumbling rock.

The last time I was in Tampa it was to address all the gay businessmen in Florida – as someone recently remarked, a room full of sodomites in suits. This time it was to introduce *Resident Alien*, which was part of Tampa's Gay and Lesbian Film Festival. The cinema manager hit on the hilarious idea of my coming into view of the audience by sitting beside the organist who arose through the floor playing a shaky version of 'Rule, Britannia,' on the huge cinema organ. It must be one of the last of those Jurassic instruments still in existence.

Tampa is a strange city, almost devoid of inhabitants. When my escort kindly drove me to a broadcasting station at the very edge of town, we overtook a bus on which there was only one passenger, and, apart from her, we saw no one. The radio station was a small shack in a jungle and was manned by a staff of beach-combers. They were very kind to me, but it was a slightly eerie experience. Needless to say, I now have a cold caused by travelling from chilly Manhattan to warm Texas back to New York, then almost at once to steamy Tampa and home again. It will pass.

My hosts from Dayton have invaded New York and taken me to Radio City to see Miss Midler. Her show is long, lavish and lewd. It was exactly what the audience should have expected, but apparently some people left in a marked manner because of the raunchiness of her jokes. Every possible bodily function was mentioned.

We sat in what in happier times would have been called the 'upper circle' and saw Miss M, as she would say, 'from a distance'. Naturally, she looked tiny, but the surprise was that she is now so thin – a fact on which she commented with pride. We attended this performance towards the end of its run, and inevitably Miss M's voice was a little tired, but her spirit – a kind of bawdy valiance – remained undiminished. I think it was this quality that so obviously appealed to the audience: they applauded every song as soon as they recognized the first few bars. Miss Midler is the archetypal music-hall artist.

I have been back to Montclair in the middle of New Jersey to attend a screening of *The Naked Civil Servant*, which was being shown to a heap of lesbians and gay men in a building attached to a Unitarian Church. By now I am accustomed to this incongruity. A transvestite once told me that if ever I found myself unaccompanied in a strange town (which heaven forfend) and wished to meet a bunch of homosexual people, I should make for the Unitarian church. The screening in Montclair was very pleasant and I sat through the movie without becoming restless.

I have also seen a secret screening of *Zelda*. This is a picture about Mr and Mrs Fitzgerald, a subject in which I am deeply interested and which, as far as I know, has never before been treated in a movie. Someone once said of this famous couple, 'They didn't want elegant surroundings; they didn't want witty companions; they just wanted something to *happen*.' This film accurately depicts their lust for excitement. For instance both Scott and Zelda jump off the roof of their house into their swimming pool while all their guests scream at them that it is too dangerous. He survived his lifelong sensation safari by taking to drink; she succumbed and went mad. The film, directed by a Mr O'Connor, makes it clear that if Fitzgerald didn't actively drive his wife insane, he certainly made no effort to save her. He is played by Mr Hutton, who looks just right and acts well, but has no natural charm and therefore cannot be seen gradually losing it. She is portrayed by Miss Richardson, who is too large for the part. In movies, if you are a victim, you have to be small. Nevertheless she is fascinating to watch. It is her film, and she never lets the audience off the hook. The weakness of this picture lies in the direction or possibly in the script. The camera does not go inside Mrs Fitzgerald's skull: we do not see her hold on reality gradually weakening. When finally she thinks she sees a huge spider walking across the piano, the hallucination seems too sudden.

After the screening, to which I went alone but at which I met a young woman who seemed to know me, the two of us, with some trepidation, attended a party at the Algonquin Hotel. There we were asked if we would like to sit among the VIPs. Never having been a VIP, I was eager to bask for a moment in their rarefied atmosphere. First I was photographed with a gentleman about my own age who turned out to be Douglas Fairbanks; then I sat beside a lady who proved to be Miss Warrick – Citizen Kane's first wife. When we were asked to be photographed together, to my delight she sent up the whole absurd situation by holding between us a few lilies from a vase on her table. I tried to look virginal.

Since then, growing ever more brazen, I have attended two fashion shows. At the first of these, I had the audacity to totter along the runway among a regiment of women wearing see-through shifts and silver boots. At the second show, I behaved a little better and remained a spectator. The models were glorious creatures, who paced to and fro in dresses no one would ever wear and kinky shoes. They moved at a brisk pace, always keeping at least two girls in view at any one time. At the end of this event, the designer, a Mr Oldham, appeared looking like a schoolboy, shorter and a little wider than any of his victims.

In the same week, never letting go of my shaky hold on the high life, I went to the Ambassador Gallery on Spring Street to the opening of an exhibition of the art work of Mr Tony Curtis. He is America's answer to Mr Matisse. When I told him this, he admitted that there is in his work a little Matisse and added, 'A little Matisse goes a long way.' He is a really nice guy. When Miss Miles (who, of course, was at both Zelda and the Ambassador Gallery) introduced me to him with the words, 'Do you know Quentin?' Mr Curtis replied, 'Yes. We were in a movie together.' There was no hint that he was one of the stars and I was an extra. This is American democracy at its best.

I nearly strayed beyond the limits of my newfound VIP-hood when I was invited to the first night of a play entitled *Any Given Day*. It is by Mr Gilroy, advertised on the invitation as a Pulitzer Prize winner. I was frightened, but I went. The play is truly Pulitzer material; that is to say it is grim. By this I do not mean that *Any Given Day* is bad. I mean that things do not turn out well for anyone on the stage. For instance, a bride and groom part on their wedding day. (Mr Pulitzer does not like happiness.) The audience was also Pulitzer material. It contained a lot of bespectacled men with thinning hair waving to other bespectacled men with thinning hair. I took them to be critics employed by conservative newspapers.

The invitation to this impressive event included supper at Sardi's restaurant. I realized that I was insufficiently Pulitzer to attend, so, when I left the theatre, I walked determinedly in the opposite direction from Sardi's but, almost immediately, I came face to face with the young woman with whom I had gone to the Algonquin only a few days previously. 'Come with us,' she cried. 'Free food.' And she led me to a huge place on Broadway. We managed to slink past a few members of staff and were given plates of food. When I had eaten everything in sight, I crept out into the gaudy night of Broadway. Fortunately, no one asked my opinion of the movie that my companion had just seen.

Finally, I have seen *Philadelphia* at a screening for the cast and crew of the film. Before it began, Mr Demme arrived, greeted his mother, and apologized for some fault that no one noticed in the print we were about to watch. When I was an extra in the party scene of this picture, I thought I was in a jolly film. I was wrong.

Philadelphia is one of the most tragic pictures I have ever seen. It concerns a court case brought by Mr Hanks against his employers because they have dismissed him, pretending he is incompetent but really because he has AIDS. He wins his case but loses his life. The lawyer defending him is Mr Washington, who, to the naked eye, seems slight but, to the camera, is monumental. He is a truly great actor. As with Miss Garbo, filming him is like photographing thought. With the use of a few words, we see him start out hating homosexuality and end up at least sorry for Mr Hanks.

Winter

*

My body was handled as though I were already dead

Mr Claus and I have never been on the best of terms. At this time of year, I tend to hide from the public scrutiny that on other occasions I cultivate. Even so, I enjoy receiving Christmas cards. A newspaper, the name of which I forget, has telephoned to ask me what was the best and what was the worst Christmas present I had ever received. There are, of course, no worst presents because no generosity must ever be disparaged. However, I do remember imploring an unknown woman, who used to telephone me in the middle of the night, *not* to send me any useless emblem of Yuletide. In spite of this prohibition, she caused me to trudge through the snow all the way to the post office to collect an evergreen wreath which weighed a ton and which I had no means and no intention of hanging in my very small room.

The most unexpected gift of this year was twelve bottles of champagne sent to me by Mr Naim Attallah, who recently interviewed me for a magazine called *The Oldie*. I had never heard of Mr Attallah, but when I mentioned his name to some friends who had just arrived from Britain for a glimpse of happiness in New York, it transpired that, over there, he is well known.

Occasionally, the pseudo-contemplative life into which I retreat at this time of year has been punctuated by telephone calls from various English newspapers expressing indignation that I have presumed to record an address to the nation to be broadcast on Christmas Day at the same time as Her Majesty's annual speech. I have refrained from quoting Miss West, who, when told her radio programme was obscene, replied, 'They could've turned it off.'

While hiding from all the jollification, I have read a number of books. The most recently received was called *Masked Culture*, published by Columbia University Press. It says that it is our duty to take part in Halloween parades and to try and ensure that they are celebrations of gender ambiguity. The text is serious – nay, philosophical – but the illustrations are outrageous, a strange combination.

A long time ago, I received a copy of *The Diary of Jack the Ripper*. Now, at last, I have read it. The author is at great pains to establish the authenticity of the manuscript. Chemical tests and other procedures have been applied to it, none of which had any interest for me. I have never paid more attention to television dramas because they were based on actual events. What is absorbing about *The Diary* is the life of Mr Maybrick, who, the book claims, was Mr Ripper. He was a cotton merchant who became an arsenic addict. I had always thought that if you gave anyone a teaspoon full of this stuff, he dropped dead on the spot. It seems that I was wrong. In happier times, men took repeated doses of arsenic to increase their potency, but it was so habit-forming that it became impossible either to continue or to desist from taking it. In the end, Mr Ripper died of this practice, but his wife was accused of murdering him. Her trial was sensational and was the most egregious miscarriage of justice imaginable. Mrs Maybrick, a pretty American woman, was condemned to death. Her sentence was later commuted to life imprisonment and she served fifteen years, emerging at the age of forty-one. This is a tragic but fascinating story.

One of the strangest episodes of my life occurred the other day. I was sitting innocently in my room when the phone rang and an unknown voice said, 'We can't get in. There are no front doorbells.' (This is because I live in a rooming house. Traditionally, in Manhattan, to live in a rooming house is to be part of an enclosed order.) It was the police. I was very frightened, but I was brave. I went downstairs, opened the front door, and three young policemen burst in. They stood about in my room (there is only one chair) and talked among themselves, but searched my living space for signs of sin. While they were doing this, the telephone rang again and a voice said, 'The ambulance is here.' I disclaimed all knowledge of such a request having been made, but went downstairs a second time. In the street, I found my landlord, half the denizens of the Lower East Side, and a Mr Sorrentino, who is a performance artist famous for imitating Elton John. I talked for some time, smiled and nodded at the assembled throng, until one of the policemen said, 'It is snowing,' and suggested (forcefully) that we board the ambulance. So I, one policeman, and Mr Sorrentino were whisked away to hospital in no time.

Once there, my arrival was treated as though long-awaited, but never welcome. My body was handled as though I were already dead, flung unceremoniously on to a wheeled stretcher, raced into an elevator where the other passengers stared down at me coldly, making me long to reach a bed where I thought my privacy would be restored. How wrong I was! Once I was turned on to my bed like a bale of shorn grass, a nurse stripped me of my clothing, which included two bandages around my ankles (without even asking why they were there), and threw them in the rubbish bin. Then she seemed interested in my pair of small white underpants and their contents. When I retreated from this prurient intrusion, which shocked modesty, the fiend, with shrieks of Filipino glee, said she thought I was wearing diapers . . . as if that made any difference!

I have often wondered why a young woman would adopt such an ugly career as that of hospital nurse. Now I know. They are penis-choppers. They only wish to spend their days among people who are physically unprotected and weaker than they. I have never known such sadism. She jabbed me with needles and, when I began to scream, said with feigned surprise, 'I understand you would rather take this stuff orally' – as if preferring to swallow a small black pill to having its contents passed into the veins of my arms were one of my funny little ways.

Now that the episode is mercifully over, I still don't know how or why it happened. I still don't know who rang for an ambulance, or what was supposed to be wrong with me. All I know is that when there is anything wrong with you, go to a faith healer, go to a witch doctor, go to a herbalist, go to a chiropractor, go to an analyst; but don't go to hospital.

As if calling on me to define my politics, I returned home to find a letter waiting for me from the *Sunday Times* of London, asking me to review a book called *The Politics and Poetics of Camp*. This is a collection of abstruse essays by the crowned heads of academia. Miss Sontag is, surprisingly, not among those contributing. It was she who elsewhere suggested that such an enterprise was in itself a form of camp.

But who is the book for? Not other professors; it is too frivolous. Not other gay readers; it is too serious. Even the cover of the book is misleading. It is a soft cover edition showing a photograph of a young man posing on top of a malachite pillar, wearing nothing but a jock strap while, with his back towards you, another young man, also wearing a jock strap – inferred by the hazardously thin straps that can just be discerned running round his hips and between his buttocks – kneels at the foot of the pillar in an attitude of adoration. It is innocent. Only Senator Helms could take exception to it. All the same, this book could not be read on a subway train.

What *are* the politics of camp? In England, it is a three-dimensional word: a verb meaning to behave in a deliberately or unconsciously effeminate manner; an adjective meaning displaying one's effeminacy in possessing it, wearing it, doing it; an abstract noun signifying the intention to display one's effeminacy. In the Twenties, it was a secret word used by low-life street people. By the Forties, it had been taken up by the theatrical profession – well known by the English public to be of dubious morality (unless you played Shakespeare) – to mean a style of acting that could be seen by the audience to be acting (or, more accurately, a style in which the actor can be seen enjoying acting). Now it means anything done not for the intrinsic value of the action, but in order to demonstrate one's individuality in doing it – showing off.

Politics, being the art of making the inevitable seem to be a matter of wise human choice, is therefore a form of camp. This homosexuals perceive and applaud because they are not involved in the process, or indeed in anything. A homosexual is standing on the bank watching other people swim. So, as far as I'm concerned, there can be no *Politics* in *Camp*, and what am I to say to the editors of the *Sunday Times*?

Whatever those Filipino fiends spent so many agonizing hours pouring into my veins in hospital I do not know, but it has shattered my memory. Twice in one week I have forgotten to take my keys with me into the outer world and have been compelled to ask our concierge to let me into my own room in the middle of the night. He is what Katherine Mansfield would call a man without a temperament and never complains, which makes me feel more ashamed. I forgot my teeth and brought humiliation to Beef Steak Charlie's. I forgot my money and was driven to roll on the floor in squirming self-abasement at the feet of the ruler of our local diner because I couldn't pay for my lunch. I forgot my 'bus money' and had to take a taxi all the way to 60th Street to the Church of St Paul the Apostle, where a memorial service was held for Jack Eric Williams.

I arrived in a rage. But my mood soon thawed in the cosiness of the situation. St Paul's is a huge church, hideous, and in a constant state of being repaired. A few people, some of whom I knew, were gathered together. They sang some of Mr Williams' songs and reminisced informally about the deceased. I kept quiet for once. There was not the embarrassing whitewash job that you might expect to prevail at such an occasion, but I didn't recognize

Mr Williams in any of the portraits painted by his students and collaborators. They described him as cantankerous and difficult on the debit side and as boyish to his credit. To me, though he was at least thirty years my junior, he was fatherly, quiet and amenable – even when I said music was a mistake. (Mr Rorem said the remark was sweeping.) To me, he was like a slow-moving bear of a man, constantly eating. One thing I would have agreed with his friend about was his brazenness. He kissed my hand in a well-lighted restaurant, but I couldn't have mentioned that in a church, however Unitarian.

I mention all this at some length because it supports the oft-repeated opinion that we all present different aspects of our personality to different people. So far, I have disagreed with this. I never caught myself doing it and would be deeply shocked if I did, but Mr Williams evidently did. He was a master at it.

The only good that has come from all this wintry weather is that it inclines one to stay indoors and therefore to work. I have written for *The Hungry Mind*, a slightly arty magazine published in St Paul, a piece about role models. The phrase didn't exist when I was young, so originality flourished. Now uniformity is all the rage because everyone is encouraged to be like someone else, the future is held captive to the past since models must be sought in history, and the great must be trimmed – nay, 'Bobbitted' – to fit some standard that children have of adults (or are supposed to have) by thin-lipped magistrates who are for ever telling famous people who come before them that they cannot drink or take drugs or sleep around or kick policemen's shins because they are 'role models to the young' (a position they never sought). This is precisely the Louis B. Mayer fallacy that the talented must be pure. In short, role models are a mistake.

But I did go out into the snow. I went to the Museum of Natural History to my first Jurassic party. This event was in celebration of the Grammy Awards. I have no idea how I got mixed up with Time-Warner, but someone I did not know was desperate for me to attend. Two charming young people came to fetch me in a purring limousine and took me through the snowy night to Central Park West. There the police and the photographers were gathered together. An unknown man, addressing me by name, led me along a white canvas tunnel into the entrance hall, where the brontosauruses greeted me. They were the only animals who knew me. We wandered through a solemn crowd of people dressed in black drinking and talking, elderly men in faultless evening dress (high-ups in the offices of Time-Warner), black women (singers), black men (orchestra), and very black men (drummers). I recognized no one and was greeted warmly only by the catering staff. The talk was all about Mr Sinatra having been cut off (not Bobbitted), but he is no longer a Time-Warner star, so it mattered little. When we left, we discovered standing on the kerb the huge man who had invited me. We were photographed together to his great satisfaction and my bewilderment – an enigmatic tableau. I reached home at half past two.

Miss Miles was not at the party.

Who is Tom Stevens? A cosy male voice at the other end of the telephone wire asked me if I knew him. I replied that I did not remember the name, but that was no reason to suppose I didn't know him intimately. I was born, I explained, with Alzheimer's disease. The voice then asked me what I did for a living. I replied that I was in the profession of being. I had to repeat that several times. Mr Stevens, the voice then said, had my name, telephone number and address in his pocket when he was arrested. This piece of news aroused my curiosity. I envisaged living my whole life on the telephone like Miss Stanwyck in Sorry, Wrong Number, but there have so far been no other calls relating to this intriguing incident. Mr Stevens was described as a heavily-built man with red hair. I nearly cried out, 'Ooh, another lovely man already!' but thought this might confuse the issue. I remained by the telephone fearing to miss the next instalment and because it was then so cold outside.

The snow brought out the best in everybody – except me. When I stood tottering on top of a pyramid of ice, hands reached out to help me down. People say that New Yorkers are indifferent to strangers. I have not found this to be so. I would say that everyone in this metropolis who isn't shooting you is your friend.

1994

Spring

*

I once told Comrade Nureyev that the charm of ballet was that someone might break his neck

In all big cities, I suppose, there is a fringe theatre. In London, it is called 'Fringe Theatre'; in New York, it is called 'Off-Off-Broadway'. This secondary entertainment is usually too risqué (filthy) or too cultural (boring) to be presented at great expense to the public, which will reject it, but it serves the purpose of employing actors, set designers etc., and prevents them from becoming desperate. Now nothing can possibly be too risqué for modern audiences, so 'kinky' has become the mainstay of fringe theatre.

Mr John Glines has established a cartel in kinkiness at the Courtyard Theater on Grove Street. I went there to see four 'gay' plays gathered into something called *Adjoining Trances* by a Mr Buck. This is very different from its last theatrical offering, which was a hilarious play about a televangelist tempted by the devil, who appears in drag for this purpose. The present play is a sober affair, an imaginary conversation between Tennessee Williams and Carson McCullers. It is only gay in that we know both parties were homosexual. It is cultural in that nothing happens. We see both writers sitting at their typewriters struggling with the strain of composition, which they endeavour to alleviate by the use of alcohol and pills. Finally, Mrs McCullers passes out and is carried by Mr Williams to a place where she can rest. The play's virtue is that it presents the extraordinary tenderness with which Mr Williams regarded women, unlike so many gay men who think of them as rivals – even enemies.

From there to Wings Theater to see *In a Land Far Away* by Mr Jefferies, who rules the place. This is a musical about the fall of Troy, with an emphasis on the 'alternative' relationship between Achilles and Patroclus. The lyrics contain rhymes that would please Mr Sondheim (there can be no higher praise). Achilles is made to rhyme with 'This place gives me the willies' and 'We're in a fix' with 'The River Styx'. The actors sing themselves to bits. They should have been warned that the space at Wings Theater is, to say the least, intimate, and they could have spared their tonsils or whatever part of your anatomy you use for singing.

Finally leaving the fringe for a real cinema, I saw *Serial Mom*. It features a real movie star, Miss Turner, and is the part she was born to play. She looks so pretty and she is so tough. In this film, she flings herself with the utmost gusto into a series of murders of anyone who disappoints or thwarts her. She is caught, but in an uproarious court scene provokes, or seduces, all witnesses who give evidence against her into behaving badly, and she is acquitted. Of course, since this is a John Waters film, the murders are as gruesome as can be, with blades withdrawn from victims dripping with blood and entrails. Even a fly that she swats is shown smeared across a plate.

After the secret screening of this picture, the entire audience was invited by *Paper* magazine to a party at Match, an unmarked grave on Mercer Street. There I found Mr Waters buried among his fans. It is always a delight to see this master of degradation looking like the head assistant in a boys' outfitters shop, dressed in a conservative suit, a sleek hairdo, and a pencil-thin, pencilled-in moustache.

It might seem from the foregoing that I have had no time to venture into the real world, but I went to the State College of Pennsylvania. I made the journey by plane – or, rather, by planes, first boarding a real flying machine to Philadelphia, and from there by a small plane made of oiled silk and matchbox wood which I found standing in a field at the airport. The passengers could feel this frail toy fighting valiantly with the elements to gain height. It succeeded and landed shakily in a town built purely to house the college and inhabited entirely by students and professors.

In addressing them, I told them that education was for teachers, not for students, and that nothing worth knowing could be taught. As usual, they remained calm. I realized that I am becoming like Miss Madonna. The more desperately I try to shock, the more hopelessly routine my act becomes.

Mr Roddy McDowall, who seems to bounce from side to side of the continent like a shuttlecock in a game of badminton, returned to New York from Los Angeles recently and took me to lunch at Sardi's. Like all restaurants in this city, though crowded to overflowing at night, it is empty at lunchtime. Nevertheless, he spotted Miss Tammy Grimes in the distance and rushed to her table to greet her in the theatrical tradition for which the place is famous. He had chosen Sardi's because it is almost next door to what is now the Helen Hayes Theater, where Miss Joan Rivers was playing *Sally Marr*.

This is an extraordinary play about the mother of Lenny Bruce. (She is still living.) It is not so much a barrel of laughs as a funeral urn of laughs. Miss Rivers flings herself into the show with an air of desperation, shouting mordant one-liners at other actors, none of whom speaks. I have no idea what Mrs Marr is really like, but this performance is straight Rivers; the same appearance that we know so well, except that her hair is red, and the same aspect on which the cost of having to be funny all the time is etched. The exhaustion was real, not acted, because not even Mr McDowall could see her afterwards. She had to recover before a second performance that evening.

I have since become aware that Miss Rivers additionally participated in a made-for-TV movie in which she plays herself and is blamed loudly by her daughter (also playing herself). All comedians are desperate people, and Miss Rivers, because of her painful thinness, her harsh voice, and her tragic private – or rather, flagrantly public – life is a cartoon of a comedian. While one laughs at what she says, one weeps for what she is.

This is the American dilemma. The neon lights of Broadway lure us like moths. We dash ourselves against them again and again in search of we know not what until we have crippled ourselves, and in this desperate flight we are abetted or rather exploited by television. Television loves disaster. To watch it regularly is to be given the impression that all children are beaten by their drunken stepfathers, all schoolgirls are raped by their escorts, all policemen are corrupt bullies, all politicians are either embezzlers or lechers or both. So we live our lives courting disaster that will bring us on to the screen into the glare of the neons. To other countries, we must seem to be a nation bent on self-destruction. It is useless trying to frighten us by telling us the world will come to an end in the year 2000, because we think of such an event only as a great television play and we hope to secure a leading part in it.

In view of all this, it is no wonder that Mrs Onassis seemed in the public mind like a calm island in the midst of a raging sea. She was sanctified not by what she did, but by what she refrained from doing. The English, who think they invented class and regard all Americans as vulgar, would do well to compare Princess Diana's behaviour in the face of Prince Charles's infidelity with Mrs Onassis's discreet way of dealing with Mr Kennedy's priapic behaviour.

I was taken by my doctor to see the hundredth season of the New York City Ballet at Lincoln Center. It was a huge success. However, Americans are not such balletomanes as the English, whose fatuous enthusiasm was parodied by Miss Gingold, who, as a ballet-goer in a revue, said, 'I clapped right from the end of *Swan Lake* to the beginning of *Sylphides.*' The audience at Lincoln Center was large and enthusiastic, but sane. The ballets were stripped to the minimum. There was no glitter – no fairy princesses, no distraught princes. The dancing was energetic but not breathtaking. I once told Comrade Nureyev that the charm of ballet was that someone might break his neck. At the Center there were no fantastic leaps – no dangerous lifts. If I sound disappointed, that is because the ballet is for the very young. Years ago I loved it, though I can't now remember whether I loved the ballet or loved loving it. I was full of aesthetic pretensions, and loved talking ballet jargon loudly in public places. All that is ended now. I am a self-made Philistine.

Onward and upward, I have flown into the presence of a Mrs Krim. I was invited by AmFAR, of which she is chairperson (co-starred with Miss Taylor, who was not present). Mrs Krim lives on West 69th Street in an elegance and splendour I have never seen rivalled. I trod over carpets as thick as pampas grass up a spiral staircase to two spacious rooms on the first floor. There were gathered tall thin men in dark suits with collegiate ties. Food was served to us by handmaidens in black dresses. The delectables offered were arranged so meticulously that I trembled to destroy the symmetry of the layout by subtracting from it. The occasion was a commemoration of the death of Mr Mapplethorpe, whose foundation has given a million dollars to AmFAR. (How did he ever get so rich?)

In a high clear voice, Miss Sischy, editor of *Interview* magazine, described to the assembled guests some of Mr Mapplethorpe's photographs in painful detail, including a picture of someone thrusting his fist into someone else's rear end. The young men did not blush, or giggle, or faint. I very nearly did all three. Like Mr Bruce, by dying, Mr Mapplethorpe has become one of the saints of pornography – a title you can only earn in this decade in this city.

Summer

*

Never open a letter written on pink paper

I have received a letter written on pink paper. Never open a letter written on pink paper. Furthermore, it was from a woman called Francesca. Another bad sign. Obviously her real name is only Frances – if not Lizzie or Ruby or worse. She claimed to have been an art student when I was a model and hankered to be remembered, though that was fifty years ago, and she was one of up to twenty students a day for thirty-nine weeks a year. She cited various touching incidents that would jog my memory – for example, she bought me cups of coffee in the mid-morning breaks – in return for which, she now wanted me to meet her at La Guardia airport. There are no free coffee breaks.

I positively refused to flaunt a card besmirched with the word FRANCESCA, but I have other means of making myself conspicuous, and I stood at the entrance to the baggage claim area. She recognized me instantly. We went to Days Hotel on Eighth Avenue, and up to her room. There, though she was so small as to be hardly visible to the naked eye, she seized me in an iron grip and demanded that I kiss her. At this point, I must remind you that we are both English and that physical contact is an embarrassment among married couples, let alone perfect strangers. I lay my cheek-bone against hers in the manner adopted by touring actresses when greeting people they do not know, and left hastily.

The next day, though she is at least seventy and I am at least eighty-five, undaunted by my coldness, she demanded that I cuddle her. 'Don't press your luck,' I warned her. She said she won't. But she will.

Yet she is not a fag-hag. Fag-hags are all plump, sophisticated, middle-aged ladies who use a lot of outmoded 'gay' gestures and utter all the traditional 'gay' catchphrases at parties where they are the only female present. This woman is worse. She is artistic, loves animals (which is always a fatuous claim, as some animals are lovable and others are downright fiendish), does not want sex but likes to stand as near the edge of the cliff as possible. Naturally she took me to the ballet – not to the same company as that which I had watched only a week before with my doctor, but next door in a theatre that was just as full. We saw *The Red Shoes*, dazzlingly staged. I was interested to see that the mechanics were at work even in this dusty backwater of art, and I imagine that all the high jinks would shock true balletomanes – the prima ballerina on wires, the red shoes dancing eerily by themselves in a spotlight, and so on, but my companion, though cultural as hell, seemed not to mind.

Is it not amazing that two theatres next door to one another, both five tiers high, should be full on the same evening in New York?

I have also seen *An Inspector Calls*, where the set received a round of applause when the curtain went up. Perhaps in view of this, I should mention that it was the work of a Mr MacNeil. It is truly impressive and actually takes part in the play, expressing the dramatist's personal views. J.B. Priestley was a Yorkshireman, which is not only to say that he came from Yorkshire, but that he shared all that county's prejudices. He was a no-nonsense man, who held that the poor were more 'real' than the rich. In this play, we see poor children playing in the rain-drenched streets and the rich eating, drinking and laughing smugly in an ornate, warmly-lighted interior. Towards the end of the drama, the lower middle class invades this interior silently, an underlying wish of Mr Priestley.

The set is so elaborate that much of the action of the play takes place in the street, obliging the lady of the house to throw herself down in the gutter, which seems a little unlikely, but no matter. It was all high drama and greatly appreciated by the audience.

Gay men are like the children of the damned: if you tell one of them anything, spontaneously the whole bunch knows it. Having whispered to someone that I didn't watch basketball because the men who play it are pathologically tall people with huge hands and feet, I was invited to an upper room on West Third Street, where the 'gay' basketball team was gathered together, to see for myself that they were of normal height with itty-bitty hands and feet. As they play against one another, this will not be a disadvantage, but in the great big outer world, they would never win. They take no exercise other than walking up five flights of steep stairs and twitching invitingly to rock music. Perhaps the hoop is lower in 'gay' basketball.

When, like Mr Alexander (the Great), you run out of worlds to conquer, you invent a perfume. I would claim that they all smell alike, but, when I took a taxi up Park Avenue, the driver said, 'Somebody's wearing Joop.' I was accompanied by two other passengers who denied the charge, so it was up to me to say, 'Forgive me, driver, for I have sinned and am no more worthy to be called thy passenger.' So they *are* all different and easily recognized. Now Mr Klein has concocted 'CK1' and a lot of men and women foregathered on Mr Roosevelt's Island, in a studio so large it would have been possible to film the Charge of the Light Brigade, to advertise this mysterious scent. No one held a glass bottle of quaint design under his nose, dilated his nostrils, and shut his eyes in feigned ecstasy or any of that rubbish. We huddled together, talking airily of this and that, while a half-naked young man crawled between our feet. It is a politically correct perfume: it is for everybody, but more than that I cannot say.

All that seems to have happened in another life, though it occurred only last week. Since then, I have been plunged into social activity so hectic that I would describe the intervening time as the worst week in my life if it didn't seem ungracious. I went to the Supper Club to watch a cabaret act staged in my honour by *Paper* magazine, starring Joey Arias, who appeared on platforms that double his natural height, and a black dress so tight that I was reminded of the words uttered by Danny La Rue at the opening of his own drag show: 'I bet you're wondering where I've put it.'

Some time ago, I posed in a white suit provided for me by a photographer who wished to take a picture of me thus clad seated in an armchair (which he carried on his head to a stagnant pool in the middle of Central Park). There I sat trying to look like a Twenties academician's illustration of a poem by Tennyson – languid, mournful, effete. He gave me the suit and at the time I wondered when I could possibly wear it but, as the hottest June broke over us like a bowl of warm molasses, I thought, 'This could be the time.' It paid off. In it, I sat in a restaurant on Second Avenue and was complimented by a middle-aged lady. 'You remind me of Quentin Crisp,' she said. I simpered, lowered my eyelids, and sighed, 'We all try to dress like him. He was such a wonderful role model.'

I was invited by Mr Origlio, the most ingenious publicist in the world, to The Ballroom. As a stunt to advertise a forthcoming play, adapted from a book by Mrs Fuller called *Me and Jezebel*, about a month-long visit by Miss Davis to the author's home, a Davis look-alike competition was being held. You would have thought that there would be a line all the way down Eighth Avenue for such an event, since none of us can be restrained from going into his act when the lady's name is mentioned, but there were only five contestants. One was very good and managed to waddle across the stage on her heels to a tee, but no one spoke with her mouth worn upside-down, which is the trademark of what one might call Bette Noire. The play should be a riot, because the book is very funny. I didn't see it, because I was sent to San Francisco.

I went with some trepidation, because it is the only city where I have received bad notices. This is because the gay population of that city seemingly cannot understand my refusal to be an apologist, much less an evangelist, for homosexuality. Nonetheless I went, and explained yet again that I was hired to be there and that my function was to sell theatre seats. Furthermore, I noted that in my opinion a theatre-goer was a middle-brow, middle-aged woman with a broken heart and it was to this vast body of people that I addressed myself. Homosexuality was never mentioned.

Disaster struck. I had been hired by a charming woman called Miss Olsen. She knew what to expect. I was but a small part of an event called Unity Expo. I think it was her object to stage a gay show to which real people were invited. I applaud this idea. It is useless to put on a gay show which is attended only by gay people. It is more of the separate-but-equal rubbish. Unfortunately, Miss Olsen's scheme did not work.

There was no publicity. No one interviewed me except one radio channel, and that was aired only when the event was safely over. Only one person photographed me. He arrived with his daughter (aged about two) in his arms. While he operated his camera, she picked his nose, smoothed his hair, repositioned his spectacles. In spite of her attentions he remained firmly focused, but I do not think the pictures were for immediate use. No one knew that I had arrived – except all the waiters in the cafés near the Cartwright Hotel where I stayed. I think that it was due to them that anyone came at all to the Fashion Center where the Expo was held. It is a huge building on Eighth Street like a luxury liner inside-out, five decks high, and with a floor space at least a thousand feet across. The basement was occupied by a sort of fair with all the usual mountebanks present – offering strange liquids said to be life-enhancing, telling fortunes, and administering invigorating rituals by laying their hands on your solar plexus. Everyone except Sylvester Stallone's mother was present.

That was all great fun. It was on the ground floor that the trouble started. In a huge auditorium, a sea of empty chairs was aligned before a small stage on which, presumably, on happier occasions, unknown fashion models strutted and swished. On the evening I was there, performers read the works of unknown writers. There was a real actor who read a real short story. I stumbled through what I think it would be polite to call an allegory by a Miss Russ.

Public readings are always a mistake. You focus your eyes on the printed page and not on the audience. I remember that, at school, it was during the classes when the master read to us from a dreary textbook that we all went to sleep, giggled, or tampered with the boy sitting next to us. When the teacher addressed us directly, we listened or at least sat still. On the stage there was a microphone. When you look at the page before you, your lips are not oriented towards the microphone. When they are, you cannot remember a word of what you have just seen and so fail to convey its meaning to a bewildered audience.

That was on Saturday. On Sunday evening a huddle of gay men attended, and I must say they were very appreciative. They were eager to ask questions. One person wanted to know if I had ever desired to have a family of my own. That startled me and the rest of the audience. I had never been asked that before. The idea of family life looms large in the minds of everyone in America, but everyone must know how awful family life is. The trouble with children is that they are not returnable. You take them out of the box and they say 'Dada' and 'Mama' and all is well – for a while. But they grow up to be larger than you are and to hold views with which you disagree.

In my book *Manners From Heaven*, I wrote that bad manners begin at home. A televisionary called Mr Boggs questioned this statement, but when I asked him if, in adult life, he had ever been so continuously and acrimoniously insulted as he had been by his brothers when he lived at home, he bowed his head. I rested my case. Not only are all the wounding words used by our siblings, but all the grimmest murders are perpetrated by relatives of the victim. Yet no one in America realizes this fact or reacts wisely

to it. The one place you cannot send runaways is home. As Miss
Stanwyck has remarked, 'Home is where you go when you run
out of places.' I can endorse that statement, but, in fairness to my
family, I must admit that I was a most objectionable child.

In spite of all the foregoing remarks, I had a wonderful time in
San Francisco. The weather was perfect: no fog in the mornings,
no earthquakes in the afternoons.

Autumn

*

I have been auctioned off at Christie's

I have been on a grand tour. Firstly I visited Minneapolis, summoned thither by an Organization for Human Rights. Needless to say, that meant gay rights – not because homosexual men have more rights than other people, but because they complain so loudly and so continuously when they are deprived of them. When asked why I was there if I didn't believe in gay rights, I said, 'because I never say no to any invitation if my fare is paid.' That reply seemed to satisfy my inquisitors.

This time I really saw the city, because I was welcomed by a Mr Pufkin. (I thought it was an affectionate nickname, Poofkin, but it was his real name.) He took me in his car to see the many lakes and beautiful green parks of which Minneapolis consists. Minneapolis, like St Louis, is much more verdant than most American cities. At nightfall, we went to a real beerfest in a real beerhall with wooden walls and a stone floor such as I have only seen in travelogues of Germany. The only things lacking were the fat thighs bulging out of leather shorts and a drinking song.

On my second night in Minneapolis I was taken to a huge convention centre, where nearly a thousand guests dined and were entertained by some half-hearted dancing and some rousing speeches. It was in fact a political meeting, but that aspect of the occasion went over my head, as I do not believe in politics. From Minneapolis, I went to Chicago, and from there to Los Angeles, where I was met by a Mrs Johnson and her brother (whom I know) and taken to an even larger convention hall, where I read in a faltering voice from my autobiography to a small huddle of people who looked quite bewildered. A few more people turned up on Sunday evening and questioned me about my love life. I explained that I didn't have one and that I would never have come to America if I was still active (like a volcano) because I thought that in order to be registered as a resident alien, you had to take an oath that you would not engage in moral turpitude, which I assume means kinky sex.

After the question-and-answer session, I went to dinner with a heap of wonderful people, including a gay banker (I didn't know that such a thing existed) who has interested Wells Fargo in the finances of the gay community, and Miss Patricia Nell Warren. I had never heard of her, but she is apparently America's answer to England's Mary Renault, having written in a time gone by a novel called *The Front Runner* about a gay athlete and his male partner. She was signing copies of a sequel called *Harlan's Race* at Unity Expo. She gave me a copy, but, like a fool, I forgot to bring it home.

Miss Warren is a wonderful person, looking like a lesbian but not mannish, looking like a writer but not aesthetic. We went on a disastrous bar crawl in which each place we entered was darker, louder, and more depraved than the last one. She did not flinch, but she did not join in. She accepted compliments, but was not in the smiling and nodding racket. I regret to have to say that my patience wore out and finally I broke down and refused to be introduced to one more person. I much deplore this shattering of my image.

The following morning I rose at dawn to be photographed for an advertisement for some spectacles (which I never wear, knowing that I would be socially washed up if I did) and returned home to answer a pile of all the usual letters asking me the usual questions, such as how does one succeed in the profession of being, what do I think of AIDS, and what is Crisperanto.

*   *   *

Miss Arcade has come home with her 'world-wandering' feet, as Francis Thompson would have said. She had been publicly taking off her clothes in Australia, Scotland, Ireland, Germany and Austria with great success. Though mortally tired, she never rests. She took me to hear Mr Albee read. Having seen *Three Tall Women*, I was curious to see what he looked like. He was surprisingly mortal – almost humble. I had expected (him being a dramatist and all) that he would jump from side to side of the rostrum and back again, squeaking one line and growling the next to indicate 'dialogue', but, instead, he read a strange story about a dog which he recited in an unemphatic but audible voice. Miss Arcade says the tale was taken from one of his plays, but what an odd play it must be, for this monologue lasted at least half an hour. The event took place in Wooster Street, in one of those huge rooms that are a characteristic of New York.

When I was young, no one who visited Manhattan talked about anything but the skyscrapers. Gertrude Stein said, 'It isn't the way they rise into the sky. It's the way they spring out of the ground.' Now every city has skyscrapers – even dreary old London. What makes New York unique is that district between Houston and Canal Streets in which all the buildings contain huge rooms – not just on the ground floor, where they are art galleries, but at all levels. These huge salons have ceilings as high as churches, and beautiful dance floors, all of laths of wood the same width, polished to the same colour, and all installed on the same day. They have never been walked on.

Having heard Mr Albee in one such venue, I tottered along brick roads in a terrible state of disrepair (by which the district is also characterized) to 20 Greene Street to the Kisslinger Gallery to see the latest paintings of Mr Iain Potts. There is something very appealing about this young man. Having been told that I had said: 'When people say, "What have you got against pictures?" I reply, "What have you got against the wall?"' he has now painted on transparent sheets of plastic and hung them in the middle of the room. The walls remained their untarnished, beautiful, blank selves, like the faces of film stars.

Thy say that if you criticized the music of the late Jack Eric Williams, he took it away, altered it, and brought it back to play for your approval. In England, artists only toss their manes and say, 'You don't understand what I'm getting at,' or some such rubbish.

When not rushing about from one form of entertainment to another, I have been trying to catch up with the books that various publishers have kindly sent me. Here I must mention that I received from The Crossing Press a book by Mr Gary Stern called *A Few Tricks Along the Way*. Not having time to do more than glance through it, I replied, as I do to all publishers whose books I haven't read, 'Please feel free to quote me as saying anything that will promote the sales of this excellent book.' Most firms receiving such a letter trot out adjectives of a generally affirmative nature for my approval to which I give my royal consent, but The Crossing Press has joined those few witty enough to print my response verbatim.

The face of the Lower East Side is darkened. The restaurant in the window of which I used to sit on exhibition like a Dutch prostitute has been shut by the authorities. This not only means that I starve, but also that there is no place where I can meet all the strangers who telephone me. The system of dealing with the outer world has broken down.

There are no front door bells where I live. I don't know why. It may be a caste symbol. Apartment dwellers have bells. Roomers do not. Therefore, if I judge that the stranger calling me on the telephone is of low degree, I ask him to call me from the corner of Third Street and Second Avenue, so that I can rush helter-skelter down the stairs and jump up and down in front of the house to make myself conspicuous. If I suppose him to be of high degree, I dare not ask him to do this and suggest that we meet in the diner on Fifth Street. It was humble, but it was also the only restaurant where there was *no music*, and tape recorders could hear me. All this, it goes without saying, is so as not to invite a stranger into my room, and avoid the charge of folly when my body is found by the police with my throat and various other parts of my body slit. All these rituals are no more.

Of course, if the strange caller suggests a place of rendezvous such as a theatre or cinema, we can meet, but even that is not simple. At every event in Manhattan there are not only the people wishing to attend, but also all the people wishing to see the people attending. This produces such a crowd (in fact, almost the entire population of Manhattan) that it is difficult to find any one person – especially as, quite often, I don't know what he looks like.

There is no limit to the oddity of the invitations that I have received lately. One evening, I found myself at a farewell party for a Mr Benoit, who was going to Nevada. When I asked him what he would do there, he said he would rally the gay community. I implored him not to do that. Left alone, a gay person is hardly gay at all, but put two such people together and they are four times as gay as they were separately. Four gay people are sixteen times as gay as two, and so on. The progression is geometrical rather than mathematical. We shall have them marching down the roulette table and demanding the *rouge et noir* be changed to straight and gay.

At the party for Mr Benoit, his late employer, Mayor Dinkins, slipped quietly into the room. When I shook hands with him, I was aware that he is a kind of saint. How did he ever get caught up by the political machine? I didn't ask him, though I travelled home with him in his limousine. His term of office must have been torture for him.

I have been auctioned off at Christie's. It was the rowdiest auction ever. People came and went, waved to one another, talked to one another, embraced, kissed – all as though nothing serious was going on, but thousands of dollars were being thrown away (should I say spent?) on a week's holiday in Belize, or a photographic session with Mr Francesco Scavullo. It was all for the people of El Salvador. Who won me and what my duties as a slave will be I never found out in all the hurly-burly.

Winter

*

That's the wonderful thing about Manhattan. You are never without friends

I've gone into mourning. Jerry's Diner on Sixth Street is shut. Soon the Lower East Side will be like one of those silver-mining towns in Nevada that are now only piles of dusty planks, and I shall emerge from one of them with a battered hat with the brim turned up in front and a fuzzy beard to point a crooked finger to show travellers where once the dancing girls and the miners sang and danced and fought.

What precious substance did we mine here? I think it was diversity without pretension – a natural individuality not bolstered by claims of artistic achievement. A brand-new eating place called the Bowery Bar has opened on East Fourth Street, but that is on the other side of Third Avenue – almost beyond redemption. The first time I went there, I knew it was an important meeting and eating place because Miss Miles and the Baroness Sherry von Korber-Bernstein were there.

I went with a Professor Connolly to the Gershwin Theater to see *Show Boat*. Professors in America are very different from English purveyors of wisdom and truth. There they have pointed white beards and walk with a stoop, weighed down by their knowledge, I presume. Here they are friendly and human and what they profess is not known. When I asked Professor Newton what he professed, he replied, 'My sin.'

Professor Connolly doesn't go that far, but he is sufficiently human to know Miss Stritch, who at the moment is playing the captain's wife in *Show Boat*. What an odd play it is! The miscegenation for which it is famous takes place at the side of the stage very early in the show, and is only the means of getting rid of the two characters who were to be the stars of the show on the boat. We do not hear of them again until we reach Chicago, where the girl is singing 'He's Just My Bill'. Miss Stritch described the show as a series of pop-up cards and music, and it is. When we went round to see Miss Stritch in her dressing room, she was dressed only in a bra and panty hose. We talked for a while and she suggested that I should perform my one-man show in Canada – as a two-man show with Professor Connolly. He, to my surprise, agreed, so I'm getting my act together and I'm taking it on the road.

As a sort of dress rehearsal, I went to Barney's dress shop to take part in a literary breakfast. I was questioned by Mr Evans about Mr Wilde. When it transpired that I heartily disliked Mr Wilde, Mr Evans was nonplussed. 'You have taken the wind out of my sails,' he cried. I offered to put it back, but he declined.

The thing that I deplore about Mr Wilde was that he never came to grips with how sordid his life had become. When the names of five or six boys whom Mr Wilde knew only in Braille (they were procured by Lord Alfred Douglas and met Mr Wilde in darkened rooms in Oxford) were read out at his trial, he was still bleating about love and invoking the fair name of Mr Plato, who died a Greek philosopher and came back as a spinster's alibi. We were asked how he would fare in today's society and I said he would never be off television. Someone compared him with Gore Vidal, which I found strange. Mr Wilde was a gross human being trying to enter English society. Mr Vidal is an elegant American trying to get out of society. Mr Wilde once said there was only one thing worse than being talked about, and that was not being talked about. He was a sort of male Madonna. All this discourse took place with us sitting on a small raised dais facing inward in the middle of a restaurant full of respectable middle-aged ladies eating toast and sipping tea. For incongruity, the situation took a lot of beating.

I have sinned in accepting an invitation from a Mr Utne to address a multitude of readers of the *Utne Reader* (of which I had never heard). He sent me a letter telling me I was one of a hundred 'visionaries' and invited me to the New York Town Hall. I accepted because I never say no to anything on the grounds that, as I lie dying, I shall not regret anything that I did – only what I didn't do. But it is a sin to accept challenges you know you cannot meet. First of all, we went to the Harvard Club, where immediately I was outclassed by the furnishings. Then, after a lot of eating and drinking and speech-making, we all sauntered to the Town Hall. Really it was an august occasion on which a lot of men about my age, in rumpled suits to show they were serious-minded, spoke words of universal and eternal wisdom. Then I went on stage and endeavoured to entertain the audience on the principle enunciated by Miss Stritch that the thing to do was to get them to like me, which was beside the point when grave prophecies were being uttered about global warming (though we could have done with some of that), ozone layers, deforestation, ecology, and various forms of religion.

I have now written to Mr Utne apologizing for my trans-gression, but the harm is done. Worse than that, I have now said yes to a Mr Stevens who has invited me to go to the Young Republicans Club. When its various members discover that I do not believe in politics, blame will fall on my host and it will all be my fault. So now I publicly state that I have not a serious thought in my head and cannot be inveigled into speaking on any world-shaping or world-shattering subjects. I long ago renounced serious relationships. Now I renounce serious topics.

The trouble with whatever is written from any angle about what is loosely called life is that it has all been said before. In the days when I had the temerity to traverse the globe telling the secret of happiness to anyone who would pay to listen (an occupation that

I have now abandoned and for which I apologize), I was harshly criticized for being insincere, which I deny, and for being unoriginal, which I freely admit. I was merely domesticating the high-flown precepts of the great thinkers of the past.

I have survived February. Mr Engel, a sculptor who made me immortal in bronze, said that more suicides occurred in February than in any other month. I did not go to that extreme, but then, I was given a 'flu shot', on the instruction of Miss Arcade, by a doctor who came all the way from Connecticut to administer it. I've had a cold ever since, but I have not been to hospital or the morgue.

There have been some dark moments, it is true. I was taken to the Palladium, where it was thought that my presence would help to launch a new magazine called *Wilde*. There, amid universal gloom and incessant din, we were shown a television programme in which some unprepossessing men were trussed up like chickens and lashed by gentlemen of dubious nationality, and I was interviewed by the ubiquitous and indefatigable Mr Barry Z, who asked me what I thought of the content of the magazine. I said that I had been shocked, but that I had remained calm. Whether such remarks will help to launch or sink the periodical in question upon the treacherous seas of debauchery, I cannot say, but shortly after midnight we were allowed to leave, bewildered but relieved.

I found myself at a banquet after seeing *Uncle Vanya*. The play was at Circle in the Square, and the supper at Gallagher's. *Uncle Vanya* received bad notices from the professional critics, which was precisely what the feast at Gallagher's was designed to prevent. They complained of the ages of the various actors. Mr Courtenay (as Uncle Vanya) says that he is forty-seven, and I thought he looked it, allowing for the fact that he was playing a Russian. In the 1880s, no man took the enormous trouble to seem young, as they now do, especially not in Russia. Nothing is more ageing than living in Russia. It was the women in the play to which I took exception. Yelena should have been dreamy, self-possessed, and self-absorbed, moving about in slow, graceful dance among her admirers as women did before they regrettably decided to be people, and Sonia should be fluttery. The difficulties imposed on the cast by the performance space may account for a lot of their defects. The stage is so vast that, in order not to hold up the action, they felt compelled to run off it, making the production feverish instead of mournful. When the play was over, I ate at Gallagher's with a charming young woman whom I had met before the show while wandering about trying to find the theatre.

That's the wonderful thing about Manhattan. You are never without friends.

Quentin Crisp

The Naked Civil Servant

'Quentin Crisp is a tonic and a delight'　　　　*Guardian*

Quentin Crisp has been described as one of England's works of art; he has become a celebrity through his lifestyle, his looks and, in recent years, his habit of appearing on television.

In this funny, moving account of his outrageous youth, Quentin Crisp describes his unhappy childhood and the stresses of adolescence which led him to London. There, in bedsitting rooms and cafés, he found a world of brutality and comedy, of short-lived jobs and precarious relationships. It was a life he faced with courage, humour and intelligence.

'Mr Crisp states his alarming case so wittily and gracefully . . . The steady chirrup of Crisperanto provides shrewd comments on queers' molls and, in particular, an unforgettable account of the American invasion of wartime London – "Never in the history of sex was so much offered by so many to so few." Truly riotous.'　　　　PAUL BAILEY, *Observer*

'Brilliant, full of sardonic humour with sharp spurts of wit'
Irish Times

0 00 654044 9
£5.99

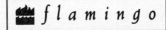 *flamingo*

Quentin Crisp

How to Become a Virgin

'His writing sparkles'   JOHN MORTIMER, *Sunday Times*

After fifty years of unalleviated obscurity Quentin Crisp
found fame at last when his autobiography *The Naked Civil
Servant* – first reviled by the public and then acclaimed –
made him a household name.

In this second volume of autobiography, peppered with tren-
chant anecdotes and polished epigrams, Quentin Crisp
describes the wider horizons of his years as a celebrity at
home and abroad, his personal philosophy of inaction and his
love affair with North America.

How to Become a Virgin is as witty, acute and perceptive as its
inimitable author.

'There must be something in a writer if every paragraph can
make you howl with mirth'   *Observer*

'If Quentin Crisp had never existed it is unlikely that anyone
would have had the nerve to invent him'   *The Times*

'Polished and deliciously shocking' GEORGE MELLY, *Guardian*

0 00 638798 5
£5.99

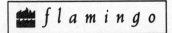

Diana Souhami

Greta and Cecil

'Greta Garbo's mysterious, inebriating allure has always defeated attempts to reduce it to words. It is no small achievement, then, that Diana Souhami has conveyed an almost palpable impression in this book of the enchantment of Garbo's beauty'
BRIAN MASTERS, *Mail on Sunday*

Greta Garbo first met society photographer Cecil Beaton in Hollywood in March 1932. At the time both were caught in turbulent same sex affairs: Greta with Mercedes de Acosta, among whose lovers were Eva Le Gallienne and Marlene Dietrich, and Cecil with Peter Watson, a wealthy dilettante. Yet Garbo flirted and danced with Beaton, told him he was pretty, presented him with 'a rose that lives and dies and never again returns' and at dawn drove away in her black Packard. Cecil took the rose home to England, framed it in silver and hung it above his bed.

Fifteen years later Greta and Cecil met again. He wrote in his diary that she closed the curtains in his rooms at the Plaza hotel, New York, and asked him if he wanted to go to bed. For her it was an idle flirtation. For him it fuelled his ambition to photograph her, to be like her and to marry her, an obsession that became a betrayal.

'We are presented with a world of wavering gender and identity, filled with reflection and reiteration, photographic images, mirrors and screens, where false façades conceal equally artificial foundations and reality is just what you break your foot on as you stumble on it in the dark'   JENNY DISKI, *London Review of Books*

'Diana Souhami sculpts the narrative to reflect her elegant ideas on the worship of images, the blurring of boundaries in love and art, and the muddle that is androgyny'   MAUREEN FREELY, *Observer*

000 655035 5
£7.99

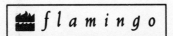

Diana Souhami

Mrs Keppel and Her Daughter

'Unnatural vices, acts of illicit passion, kings, mistresses, elopements, extravagant riches – this book has them all . . . A wonderful story, wonderfully told'　CHRISTOPHER HUDSON, *Daily Mail*

Alice Keppel and her daugher Violet Trefusis were both, in their ways, legendary lovers. Mrs Keppel, mistress of Edward VII and great-grandmother to Camilla Parker-Bowles, was the acceptable face of adultery. For Violet, romance proved tragic and destructive as her mother used all the force at her command – charm, determination, money – to repress her love affair with Vita Sackville-West.

From memoirs, diaries and letters, Diana Souhami portrays this intense mother/daughter relationship. Her story of these two women, their lovers and their lovers' mothers goes to the heart of questions about the monarchy, family values and sexual freedoms.

'Souhami set out to expose the hypocrisies and evasions surrounding upper-class sexual mores . . . the book has a genuine pathos and originality'　ANNE CHISHOLM, *Times Literary Supplement*

'This dark and Gothic tale of passion and cruelty, of an indomitable mother and a frail daughter, is all the more shocking for its imperturbable, elegant settings – Biarritz, London drawing-rooms, Florentine villas and English country houses. Electrifying and heartrending'　FLORA FRASER, *Daily Telegraph*

'Souhami has a Midas touch with words. Her narrative sparkles'
NIGEL NICOLSON, *Sunday Telegraph*

0 00 638714 4
£6.99

Marsha Hunt

Repossessing Ernestine

The Search for a Lost Soul

At the beginning of the 1920s in Memphis, Tennessee, Ernestine Hunt's future seemed bright – young, pretty, intelligent, recently married and now with three healthy sons. Yet she was to spend over fifty years in a mental institution before her granddaughter, the actress and writer Marsha Hunt, discovered she was still alive.

Her search for her grandmother's history became a quest not just for the soul of a woman but of a family, a race and a nation.

'A magnificent achievement. I was moved to tears'
VAL HENNESSY, *Daily Mail*

'No anger over the wrongs of the past could be as eloquent as this cool truth-telling. Let this book get a grip on you – you won't regret it'
JILL PATON WALSH, *Sunday Express*

'An amazing story, full of twists and turns, Dickensian coincidences and discoveries . . . *Repossessing Ernestine* is a remarkable account of a forgotten woman whose life was taken from her. The strength of this powerful, vividly written narrative lies in Hunt's detached control of her anger, her despair, her hope'
EILEEN BATTERSBY, *Irish Times*

'*Repossessing Ernestine* touches a strange, powerful, painful chord in this century of the displaced and dispossessed. It invokes a whole world of shadows'   HILARY SPURLING, *Daily Telegraph*

0 00 654875 X
£6.99